Assurance: Launch Pad for Righteous Living

Assurance: Launch Pad for Righteous Living

1 John

This inductive Bible study is designed for individual, small group, or classroom use. A leader's guide with full lesson plans and the answers to the Bible study questions is available from Regular Baptist Press. Order RBP0046 online at www.regularbaptistpress.org, e-mail orders@rbpstore.org, call toll-free 1-800-727-4440, or contact your distributor.

REGULAR BAPTIST PRESS
1300 North Meacham Road
Schaumburg, Illinois 60173-4806

The Doctrinal Basis of Our Curriculum

A more detailed statement with references is available upon request.

- The verbal, plenary inspiration of the Scriptures
- Only one true God
- The Trinity of the Godhead
- The Holy Spirit and His ministry
- The personality of Satan
- The Genesis account of creation
- Original sin and the fall of man
- The virgin birth of Christ
- Salvation through faith in the shed blood of Christ
- The bodily resurrection and priesthood of Christ
- Grace and the new birth
- Justification by faith
- Sanctification of the believer

- The security of the believer
- The church
- The ordinances of the local church: baptism by immersion and the Lord's Supper
- Biblical separation— ecclesiastical and personal
- Obedience to civil government
- The place of Israel
- The pretribulation rapture of the church
- The premillennial return of Christ
- The millennial reign of Christ
- Eternal glory in Heaven for the righteous
- Eternal torment in Hell for the wicked

ASSURANCE: LAUNCH PAD FOR RIGHTEOUS LIVING, 1 JOHN
Adult Bible Study Book
Vol. 59, No. 4
© 2011
Regular Baptist Press • Schaumburg, Illinois
www.regularbaptistpress.org • 1-800-727-4440
Printed in U.S.A.
All rights reserved
RBP0049 • ISBN: 978-1-60776-369-7

Contents

Preface

Am I really saved? What are the evidences of salvation? Can I count on eternal life?

Questions like these are critical for all believers to answer. Believers who never find assurance of eternal life are doomed to spiritual stagnation. Assurance of eternal life becomes a believer's launch pad for righteous living.

John knew the importance of assurance of eternal life as he penned the first of three epistles that bear his name. His recipients were under pressure from false teachers to change their beliefs about Christ in particular. The false teachers caused them to question their salvation. John's words helped the recipients of his letter gain assurance of eternal life so they might grow spiritually as God intended.

As you study 1 John, you will consider issues such as fellowship, obedience, love, truth, discernment, faith, and confidence. All these are presented from the perspective of one who lived close to Christ on earth. These issues are of practical concern to you as you live a "faith life" each day.

This study of 1 John will also reveal to you the marks of an authentic Christian. Those marks will help you evaluate your life for genuine faith as well as give you insight into how God expects a believer to live.

Approach this study with an open heart. And be ready to be respond to the Holy Spirit as He speaks to you through His Word.

Certain of Salvation

God wants His children to know that they are truly saved.

1 John Overview

**"These things have I written unto you that believe on the name of the Son of God; that ye may know that ye have eternal life, and that ye may believe on the name of the Son of God"
(1 John 5:13).**

Most people who consider growing to be 100 years old would like to do so only if they could still take care of themselves and carry on a lucid conversation. Marion Fields Wyllie has exceeded that expectation. She did more than carry on a conversation at 104 years old; she actually wrote a book of short stories and had it published. Marion was first published in 1919 when her poem was printed in the *Toronto Globe*. Decades later she is still continuing to write. She is known now as Canada's oldest living published author.

Getting Started

1. What is the value of reading the writings of an author who has lived a full life?

2. What is the most valuable lesson you learned from an elderly person?

The Bible advises great value is found in the wisdom of godly elders. The apostle John fits that description. Late in his life, he penned three short letters giving direction for Christian living. The book of 1 John is not only divinely inspired, it also conveys the wisdom this Christian statesman had gleaned over many years.

Searching the Scriptures

The Writer

The letter of 1 John has historically been attributed to the apostle John. It is one of the few epistles in the New Testament that does not have an explicit statement of who wrote it. Because of this, many scholars, particularly in the last century, have questioned whether the apostle John was really the author of this letter.

Consider these five reasons for concluding that 1 John was indeed written by John.

First, this was the stated belief of many of the earliest Christian writers. These writers, typically called the church fathers, lived only a few generations after John. Not all of them spoke directly to the issue, but Irenaeus, Clement of Alexandria, and Tertullian all stated clearly that John the apostle wrote 1 John. Although their testimony may not be conclusive evidence, it certainly is a strong witness that should not be ignored.

Second, in 1:1–3 the writer declared that he was an eyewitness of Jesus Christ during His earthly life. Certainly the apostle John fits this description. John was one of the earliest disciples whom Jesus called to follow Him (Matthew 4:21, 22). Throughout Christ's ministry John was in the disciples' inner circle. He was one of the few who witnessed the full range of Christ's actions. Because 1 John was written by a significant eyewitness of Christ's incarnate ministry, John has to be considered one of the most likely possible writers.

3. What significant events in Christ's life did John witness? (See Matthew 17:1–3; 26–36; Mark 5:22–24, 35–43; John 20:1–10.)

Third, there are frequent and detailed parallels between 1 John and the Gospel of John, in particular, John 13—17. Because of the great similarity between the two books in writing style and content, scholars who deny that John wrote this epistle even argue that it was written in conscious imitation of the Gospel of John. But it seems more likely that the same person wrote both books.

Fourth, the epistle has a tone of spiritual authority. John was one of the leading apostles, whom Jesus commissioned to serve in His place. Throughout 1 John, the apostle spoke with confident authority of the truth he had received and proclaimed.

4. Read John 19:26 and 27. What deeply personal commission did John receive from Jesus?

Fifth, the writer often referred to his readers as "my little children" (2:1). This is the kind of expression that a grandfather might use. His firm apostolic tone was tempered with deep compassion and affection. This language implies that the writer was an elderly, revered Christian leader. In addition, it matches portrayals of John as an old man who ministered in Ephesus.

5. Why might critics want to deny that John wrote 1 John?

The Setting

The historical setting for John's letters is hard to determine. The book of Acts details his involvement in only four episodes early in his ministry (Acts 1:13; 3:1; 4:19; 8:14). Consequently, the setting must be drawn from inferences in 1 John and the few references found in the writings of the church fathers.

Hanging heavily over 1 John is the threat of false teachers. By using John's teachings, scholars have attempted to identify these false teachers. At least three brands of error can be inferred: gnosticism, Docetism, and an erroneous view separating the human Jesus from the divine Christ.

6. Look up "gnosticism" in a dictionary. Why would gnosticism undermine Christianity at its very core? Think about the incarnation of Christ.

Gnosticism insisted that the Son of God could not have become human because that would bring the spiritual and material realms together. This false teaching would rule out Christ's incarnation and thus His substitutionary death on the cross and future reign on His millennial throne as a descendant of David.

7. How might gnosticism have affected the early Christians' assurance of salvation?

The Docetists claimed that Jesus' humanity was not real—that instead of being truly human, Jesus only appeared to take on a physical body. This false teaching emphasized the deity of Christ to the extent that it denied His humanity. In other words, He did not genuinely enter the human race and identify Himself with sinful humanity.

8. Based on Philippians 2:5–8, why was it important for Christ to become a human?

The third error stated that when Jesus was baptized, the divine Christ descended upon him but that Christ left Jesus before the crucifixion. Therefore, when Jesus died on the cross, He died as a mere human, not as the perfect God-man offering the substitutionary atonement for sin.

It is impossible to know precisely which false teaching John was countering in a given verse. In fact, it could well be that his readers were facing a mixture of overlapping and contradictory false teachings. So the focus must be kept on the truth which John set forth.

9. What was the common denominator of all these false teachings?

10. What false religions today threaten to shake a believer's understanding of and trust in Jesus Christ?

According to 1 John 2:19, some people within the Christian community had already defected to falsehood. They had moved away from the solid truth into false speculations, which had produced a spirit of arrogance in their hearts. In their self-deceit they claimed to have arrived at a state of moral perfection, in which they were no longer contaminated by sin. They doubtless urged genuine Christians to forsake simple belief in Christ to achieve a supposedly higher level of spirituality.

11. Why do false teachers bother with trying to influence believers?

Theological error often results in ethical error, because wrong belief typically produces wrong behavior. This was certainly the case with the false teachers against whom John wrote. John used strong terms such as "seduce" (2:26) and "deceive" (3:7) to describe what they were teaching.

John, therefore, used a twofold approach when writing against false teachers. On the one hand, he firmly countered the false teachings by raising solid logical and theological objections. On the other hand, he encouraged Christians to stay with the truth they had received by giving them warm pastoral reassurance.

12. Which approach to writing against false teachers did John use in 1 John 2:21–23: firm countering or pastoral reassurance?

13. Which approach is John using in 1 John 3:1–3?

The Purpose

In John 20:30 and 31 the apostle stated clearly his purpose for that entire book, but he had a fourfold purpose in writing 1 John.

14. According to 1 John 1:3, what was John's purpose in writing First John?

15. What purpose does he give in 1:4?

16. What purpose does he list in 1 John 2:1?

17. What does 1 John 5:13 say about John's purpose?

Clearly, John was addressing faithful Christians, not false teachers. So his purpose was pastoral and constructive. He spent most of his time in reassuring and warning the faithful. Knowing they were under attack, John came alongside to encourage and support them. He also warned them of the false teachers' serious threat.

Just as the threat was a mixture of false teachings, so John's response had a combination of purposes. He reassured his readers of theological truths, especially about the identity of Jesus Christ. In addition, he reminded them of the reality of sin and of God's provision for forgiveness. He also reminded them of the need to maintain fellowship with God and one another. In doing all of this, John countered the false teachers' doctrinal and practical errors.

Key Themes

First John is a very difficult book to outline, because it was not written as a theological treatise. Instead, John was responding to the urgent threat posed by the false teachers. He spoke as a spiritual father to his children. In warm yet firm tones, he repeated several key themes.

Throughout the book John brought his readers back to the foundational truths of the Christian faith. He wanted to remind them of "the old, old story" to defend them from the brand new erroneous views of the false teachers.

18. What common phrase in 1 John 1:1; 2:7, 24; and 3:11 points out John's emphasis on the foundational truths?

John wanted his readers to stand on the firm bedrock of God's truth, rather than slipping on the shifting sand of human speculations.

Numerous times John spoke of knowledge and certainty. The false teachers had raised doubts about the person of Jesus Christ, as well as other central tenets of the faith. To counter these doubts, John reminded them of what they could truly know about Christ.

The false teachers claimed to be Christians even though their teachings diverged greatly from the teachings of Christ. John devoted much of 1 John to describing three distinguishing marks of authentic Christianity: theological, moral, and social. The theological mark is belief that Jesus was truly the Son of God in the flesh. The moral mark is consistent obedience to the commandments of God. The social mark is love for one another in the family of God.

These three marks are not set forth as the way to become a Christian. Instead, they are already true of genuine Christians. Each mark requires the indwelling work of the Holy Spirit. The Spirit teaches God's truth, including a proper understanding of Jesus Christ as the unique God-man. It is the indwelling Spirit Who enables Christians to obey God and love others, because these actions and attitudes are contrary to the natural sinful bent of humans.

19. Which of these marks is the most important? Why?

The false teachers were wrong in their understanding of Jesus Christ, and their lives were characterized by disobedience and lack of love. John's readers, however, were true Christians. As they evaluated their lives in the light of the three marks of Christians, they would be reassured of their own spiritual status in Christ. This renewed confidence would in turn blunt the arrows of doubts that the false teachers shot at them.

Another prominent theme in 1 John is the vital connection between faith and love. John had little patience for people who claimed to love God but at the same time did not love their Christian brothers and sisters. He argued that godly belief must produce godly behavior. Because of that, godly behavior that expresses love for others is an accurate indicator of true belief in God. The Holy Spirit Who indwells all genuine Christians teaches them both what to believe and how to behave.

Making It Personal

20. Do you believe that Jesus in the flesh is truly the Son of God? If so, how does that belief affect your life?

21. Is your life characterized by consistent obedience to the commandments of God? On what do you base your answer?

22. Would your fellow believers describe you as a genuinely loving person? Why or why not?

If you are not sure you are saved, then take care of the matter today. Seek the help of a believer or a pastor who can tell you more about putting your trust in Christ as your Savior.

23. Memorize 1 John 5:13.

The Source of Fellowship

Fellowship with other Christians flows out of fellowship with God.

1 John 1:1–4

"That which we have seen and heard declare we unto you, that ye also may have fellowship with us: and truly our fellowship is with the Father, and with his Son Jesus Christ" (1 John 1:3).

Church bulletins are notorious for their bloopers—rightly so or not. Many times the mistakes aren't too off base. For example, "Thursday night—Potluck supper. Prayer and medication to follow." In 2008, a Baptist church held a "Beast Feast and Wild Game" potluck. Three hundred people attended the supper, with at least twenty wishing afterward that they hadn't. Those twenty became ill. Eight of the twenty, including two young brothers, were infected with E. coli. For them, the Beast Feast was unpleasantly memorable.

Getting Started

1. What memorable potlucks have you been to?

2. Why might a potluck also be called a fellowship dinner?

Churches frequently use the term "fellowship" to describe a social gathering or meal. What the apostle John meant by "fellowship" goes far beyond sharing food. In the opening paragraph of 1 John, he related truth to fellowship and drew a connection between fellowship with God and fellowship among believers. True joy comes when fellowship with God flows into fellowship with other Christians.

Searching the Scriptures

The first three verses of 1 John set the stage for the letter's major themes and purposes. From the start John wanted his readers to understand that truth is the foundation for fellowship.

3. Why is truth the foundation for fellowship?

The Witness Speaks

The main verb for verses 1–3 does not come until the final verse, when John said, "declare we unto you." Before he got to the verb "declare," John heaped up several clauses that describe his message. Each of the clauses begins with "that which" or "which."

4. Note the clauses in 1 John 1:1 that describe John's message by looking for the key words "that which" or "which." What two words would you use to summarize what those clauses say about John's message?

The five clauses in verse 1 form a progression in the intensity of observation and the certainty of knowledge. John started by referring to "that which was from the beginning"; this phrase may refer to the beginning of the gospel message that was centered in the incarnation of Christ. In other words, John spoke of the original Christian truth in contrast to the novel doctrines of the false teachers. He was writing to confirm the genuineness of the account of Jesus, because others had introduced a new but false story.

The next two clauses, "which we have heard" and "which we have seen with our eyes," speak of the more direct evidence that John observed. As one of Jesus' disciples, John for three years had listened to the Lord and watched Him. When John wrote his Gospel, he recorded these words and works of Jesus so that all might believe in Him (John 20:30, 31).

The last two clauses involve the most direct and undeniable evidence. John told of that "which we have looked upon, and [which] our hands have handled." The term "looked upon" is the same Greek verb translated "beheld" in John 1:14. Both verses speak of observation that goes beyond physical sight to spiritual understanding.

When John referred to looking upon and handling, he may have had in mind the time Jesus visited His disciples eight days after His resurrection (John 20:26–29). Jesus invited the previously doubtful Thomas to touch the wounds in His hands and side. Here was evidence that Jesus had indeed died on the cross and risen from the dead. His death and resurrection are the heart of the gospel (1 Corinthians 15:3, 4), the good news that God's own Son provided Himself as the substitute for sinners so that those who believe on Him can have salvation from sin and receive eternal life with God.

5. Is it necessary today to have physical evidence of the works of Jesus to believe upon Him? Explain.

Hold That Thought

In verse 1 John spoke of the truth that he and the other disciples of Jesus had witnessed. Before he moved on to state his purpose in verses 3 and 4, John reinforced the reality of the message he proclaimed by a parenthetical statement.

In verse 2 John explained how he had come to know the gospel message. Unlike the false teachers, who invented their teachings, John had received the truth that God had manifested to the disciples. God had made known His truth in such a way that the disciples could be eyewitnesses to it.

John had a twofold source of authority. First, he had been an eyewitness to God's revelation through Christ, so he could declare what he himself had seen and heard. Second, "show" ("shew") refers to the authority of one who has received a commission from a superior. In John's case, Christ had authorized him as an apostle to take the truth of the gospel to the entire world (cf. Matthew 28:18–20; Acts 1:8).

6. Why was it necessary for some people to view the earthly works of Jesus firsthand?

In verse 2 John described the "Word of life" (v. 1) as the eternal life that was with the Father and had been manifested to the disciples. John 3:16 and 36 and 5:24 reveal eternal life to be the divine quality of life that God gives to those who believe on Christ. It is a new kind of life that begins in the present and continues forever for those who accept the gospel. This was the truth John had witnessed and his readers needed to grasp in the face of counterfeit doctrines. Only this word of life in Christ could provide a reliable basis for fellowship and joy.

7. How do believers enjoy eternal life now?

Even though in style verse 2 is parenthetical, in substance it is a crucial element in John's argument. John forged a solid chain of truth. God designed His plan for eternal life, which involved Christ's incarnation and substitutionary death. The disciples were eyewitnesses to this truth, and then Christ commissioned them to declare it to the world. John was writing as God's authorized messenger so his readers could be reassured of the truth as they were confronted by false teaching.

Koinonia, More Than Just Greek

After the parenthesis in verse 2, John resumed the sentence with which he began the letter. He summarized the content of verses 1 and 2 in the words "that which we have seen and heard declare we unto you." Unlike the gnostic teachers, who claimed to have special knowledge that was knowable by only a select elite, John delighted in declaring God's truth to all. He knew that the gospel of Christ is good news that needs to be shared with others. Writing this epistle was one part of John's obedience to his commission as an apostle of Christ.

John then revealed his purpose in declaring God's truth to his readers. The immediate purpose was that they might have *koinonia*, or fellowship, with John and the Christians whom he represented. In the New Testament, *koinonia* speaks of common participation in the blessings of Christ. The basis for this rich fellowship is the strong bond between Christians, Christ, and God the Father. When a person receives Christ as his Savior, he enters into a relationship with God. In fact, John 1:12 states that Christians become children of God.

8. How do we develop and maintain fellowship with God?

Christians, who each have a relationship with God through Christ, also enter into the spiritual family of God's people. The union with God overflows into union with other Christians. In other words, vertical fellowship with God produces horizontal fellowship with others. As God's children, Christians have fellowship with one another because they are joined at the heart.

9. How do we develop and maintain fellowship with other believers?

The rest of 1 John goes on to explain how the gospel of Christ should set into motion rich fellowship with God and other believers. Proper belief has great practical benefits. The false teachers preached error that undermined all of that. Their wrong understanding of Christ contradicted the truth of the gospel. As a result, there was no basis for true fellowship with God or others. Rejection of the truth is a mortal blow to genuine fellowship.

In the final clause of verse 3, John insisted emphatically: "Truly our fellowship is with the Father, and with his Son Jesus Christ." True Christian fellowship, genuine Christian unity, must always be focused on God. Fellowship is not produced by external human organization.

10. Why will genuine Christian fellowship manifest itself whenever true believers are together?

True fellowship comes as a result of an internal spiritual bond. People may join together in many different associations in which they have common interests or goals, but only the shared relationship with God through Christ can produce genuine Christian fellowship. Anything else is a pale imitation.

True Christian fellowship also involves Jesus Christ. The false teachers in the first century regarded Christ as less than the incarnate Son of God. This fundamental error in doctrine prevented them from true fellowship with God and genuine believers. In the same way, how people view Christ today determines whether they are able to participate in the benefits of Christian fellowship. True fellowship is always focused on union with God through His Son Jesus. He is the bond who holds all Christians together.

11. What does it mean *not* to have personal fellowship with a church that has a deficient understanding of Jesus Christ?

12. What does it mean *not* to have corporate (church body) fellowship with a church that has a deficient understanding of Jesus Christ?

Fruit of Fellowship

As the elderly John wrote 1 John, he frequently called the readers his little children. Just as loving parents delight in seeing their children happy in doing what is right and find complete joy when their children are joyful, so John longed for his writing to bring joy to his readers' hearts.

In his opening paragraph, John connected three great realities. Verses 1 and 2 speak of God's truth that Jesus Christ had manifested to John as an eyewitness and an apostle. Verse 3 declares this truth, because it alone can produce fellowship between God and His people and among believers. Verse 4 states that in producing fellowship, truth results in joy. As his readers faced the threat of false teaching, John refocused their vision on the truth of the gospel, and he renewed their joy in the Lord.

13. Why does genuine fellowship bring joy?

14. Why would genuine fellowship with God and with other believers provide what people today crave?

Christianity is serious, because it affects every aspect of life and the eternal destiny of all people. Nevertheless, Christianity should be full of joy. As John indicated in this preface, the gospel has provided the present possession of eternal life, a quality of life that goes far beyond anything the world can offer. In addition, Christians can be joyful because they have fellowship with God the Father and with Jesus Christ. And God has provided for them the riches of fellowship with His people everywhere.

15. What are some evidences that true, joyful Christianity is present?

God wants His children to be full of joy. To do that, He has provided what people in our society vainly pursue. To people seeking security, God promises eternal life. To people seeking pleasure, God gives true joy without regrets. To people seeking wealth, He provides the riches of Heaven as an inheritance.

As John continued, he helped his readers understand why and how they could be joyful. He taught them how to move from truth to genuine fellowship so they could experience full joy.

Making It Personal

16. How would you describe your level of fellowship with God? Is your relationship with Him vital to your life? Do you actively seek to know God better?

17. What things, people, or practices are you using to try to fill any void in your life left by a lack of fellowship with God? How do these attempts affect your joy?

18. If you have a low level of fellowship with God, what steps can

you take to deepen your fellowship? Spend more time in His Word? Talk to Him more? Seek to know and do His will?

19. Memorize 1 John 1:3.

No Excuses

Fellowship is nurtured when sin is honestly confronted.

1 John 1:5—2:2

"And he is the propitiation for our sins: and not for ours only, but also for the sins of the whole world" (1 John 2:2).

What happens when you sit on a piece of unwrapped chocolate for a half hour or so? It becomes part of you! That is what a businessman embarrassingly found out. On three separate occasions a chunk of chocolate dropped from his granola bar onto his car seat while he was driving to work. Each time the chocolate smeared all over the back of his pants. And each time he didn't know it happened until he had walked around his office for an entire day. Not exactly an ego boost!

Getting Started

1. Describe a time when you noticed a spot of food or grease on your clothing at a very inopportune time.

2. How did you respond?

3. Did you ignore the spot or even deny that the spot was there? Why not?

John dealt with believers who downplayed or even denied their stains of sin. We, too, have a tendency to deal with our sins by downplaying or denying them when we should be confessing them. John's word will challenge us to take a proper view of our sin and to deal with it as God desires.

Searching the Scriptures

God Is Light

When John wrote 1 John, he had one central point to make. At the beginning of the letter, he stated this point clearly, because he did not want any of his readers to miss it. The rest of the epistle explains, expands, and applies this key principle.

In the prologue (1:1–4), John said that he was declaring "that which we have seen and heard." In verse 5 he picked up that same language as he defined the content of the message he had heard; that is, "God is light, and in him is no darkness at all."

4. How would you summarize the meaning of 1 John 1:5?

John clearly contrasted the things of God, in the sphere of light, with the things contrary to God, in the sphere of darkness. As light, God is absolutely perfect in all aspects. Darkness is opposite to God's perfections.

The contrast between light and darkness illustrates spiritual realities in numerous ways.

5. In intellectual terms, light speaks of God's truth. What opposite category would darkness represent?

6. In moral terms, light indicates purity. What opposite category would darkness represent?

Intellectually or morally speaking, God is the fixed standard against which all must be measured. Apart from God's light, mankind gropes in darkness, unable to see the right way (cf. Jeremiah 10:23).

John defined the meaning of light by both positive and negative means. Throughout the letter he indicated beliefs and behaviors that belong to God's realm of light—that measure up to God's standard of truth and goodness.

At the same time, he described beliefs and behaviors that lie outside God's realm—outside the light. Those things belong to the sphere of darkness; they do not measure up to God's perfections.

John encouraged his readers to follow the light and forsake the darkness. Just as there is no darkness at all in God, so there must be no darkness in His people.

Three False Claims

Three times in 1 John 1 (vv. 6, 8, 10), John used the phrase "if we say" to introduce a false belief that denies the message that "God is light, and in him is no darkness at all."

In each of these cases, John exposed and countered the false claim, then pointed to the death of Christ as the only sufficient remedy for sin.

7. How might a flashlight with a partially covered lens represent common views of sin?

8. Are these views Biblical? Explain your answer.

Claim One

9. Summarize the first "if we say" statement in 1 John 1:6.

The first false claim is that Christians can have fellowship with God while walking in darkness. Throughout the Bible, the word "walk" is used to speak of a consistent pattern of movement, or a lifestyle. This claim says that a sinful lifestyle does not impede one's relationship with God.

The New Testament clearly teaches that Christ has made His people free from the law. Nevertheless, as the book of Galatians argues, freedom does not mean license to sin, but rather it is liberty to please God rather than being in bondage to sin (Galatians 5:1).

Sin is a barrier to fellowship with God (cf. Psalm 66:18; 2 Corinthians 6:14). In God there is no darkness at all. Therefore, if a Christian walks in darkness, he cannot be walking with God in His realm of light. Consequently, those who make this "fellowship" claim are lying, not doing the truth. Sin destroys fellowship with God. Those who say otherwise are deceived.

In verse 7 John gave the remedy.

10. Read 1 John 1:7. What is the remedy for the first false claim?

John reinforced the importance of walking in the Spirit—in the realm of God. Instead of slipping into a lifestyle dominated by sin and error, Christians must align themselves to God's goodness and truth. They need to walk in the light as He is in the light. God must become the standard by which believers measure their belief and behavior.

Walking in darkness destroys fellowship with God and others. Being right with God provides both spiritual and social wholeness.

Walking in the light does not come about by a mere human decision. Only the blood of Jesus Christ is sufficient to cleanse people from the defilement produced by the sin nature, allowing them to "walk in the light."

Christians who tolerate sin in their lives fail to value properly what Christ did on the cross. Christ's death did more than just provide an escape from eternal punishment. It also provided the way to fellowship with God. Walking in darkness tragically discounts what Christ died to accomplish.

11. What words would you use to describe what God thinks about the practice of living in sin as a Christian?

Claim Two

12. Identify the second "if we say" phrase in 1 John 1:8.

13. How might a flashlight with a completely covered lens represent the erroneous view presented in verse 8?

The second erroneous claim is a denial of sin. This claim alleges that individuals are morally perfect and without a sin nature. Instead of facing up to the fact that sin is a continual threat, it views sin as a problem only for others.

John was quick to counter that the denial of sin is really self-deception. Those who claim to have no sin nature do not possess the truth. Their inaccurate perception comes from ignorance or pride.

People have an incredible ability to deceive themselves with regard to sin. To rationalize sinful actions and attitudes, people invent all sorts of justifications for wrong. The result is the kind of comprehensive self-deception that is unwilling or unable to admit any sin.

14. What would you say to someone who claims to be sinless?

Christians must realize that they, too, are prone to this deception. Sin is always lurking in the shadows ready to pounce and consume. Those who think they are beyond temptation need to be especially careful, because pride leads to a fall (cf. 1 Corinthians 10:12).

In 1 John 1:9 the apostle indicated the proper approach to sin. Believing that one has no sin nature is a refusal to honestly face the potential problem and is a preference for living a lie. Christians should confess sins—acknowledging their sin honestly before God.

15. How often should we confess our sins?

16. What are some practical ways to keep up to date with confessing sins?

As Christians confess specific sins to God, they can be confident of His favorable response. God is faithful and just to forgive sins and to cleanse from all unrighteousness. God's unchanging character is the guarantee of cleansing from sin.

When God forgives sins without demanding anything additional from the repentant sinner, He remains just, because He accepts Christ's payment for those sins. When Christ died on the cross as the perfect substitute for sinners, He paid the full price for sin once and for all— even providing for future sins that will be committed.

In accepting Christ's sacrifice, the Father forgives the confessed offense and cleanses the stain caused by the sin (Psalms 51:7, 10; 139:23, 24; Isaiah 1:18). Denying sin provides neither forgiveness nor cleansing; honest confession to God brings both (Proverbs 28:13).

Confession of specific sins is crucial for nurturing fellowship with God and other Christians.

Claim Three

17. Find the third "if we say" phrase in 1 John 1:10.

The words "we have not sinned" in verse 10 perhaps were intended to mean "never sinned at all." In other words, people who make this claim say they have no sin nature and are incapable of committing individual acts of sin.

The Bible is clear that sin has contaminated every human being (cf. Psalm 14:1–3; Isaiah 53:6; Romans 3:10–12, 23). According to Isaiah 53:6, all have gone astray, and the Lord laid on Christ the iniquity of everyone.

18. Read 1 John 1:10. How does our understanding of sin relate to God's holiness?

Because God's Word is clear in teaching that all people are sinners, the claim of sinlessness in reality charges God with lying. However, God's Word tells the truth, and those who deny God's Word do not have His truth in them.

Additionally, the claim of those who deny sin implies that they do not need salvation. As far as they are concerned, they are good enough for God. They believe they do not need what Christ's death provided. John answered this erroneous claim in 2:1 and 2.

19. According to 1 John 2:1 and 2. Why are we not hopeless when we sin?

Sin is a dangerous and deceptive foe, and it must never be underestimated. At the same time, John did not want believers to overestimate sin. God knows that His children will sin, and He has already made provision for them. Not only did Christ die on the cross in the past, but in the present He is an advocate for His people. When Christians sin, Christ pleads their case before the Father. There is no need to be afraid to confess sins before God, because the blood of Christ is sufficient to cleanse all sin. Christ's presence on behalf of His people guarantees a favorable verdict by God.

Verses such as Romans 1:18 show that God's righteous character cannot tolerate sin. His holiness demands that He judge sin in His righteous wrath.

Christ can plead successfully for His people because He is the propitiation for sins. "Propitiation" speaks of the complete satisfaction and removal of God's judicial wrath against sin. When Christ died on the cross, His once-for-all sacrifice paid the full price for sin. To satisfy God's just wrath against sin, Christ had to lay down His own life. God the Father accepted His sacrifice as the perfect substitute for sinners. Christ, therefore, does not argue that humans are innocent or good enough, but rather that He Himself has paid the full price for their sins.

20. How should knowing you have an advocate before the Father affect your response to sin in your life?

John went on in verse 2 to say that Christ died not only for the sins of Christians, but for the sins of the whole world. Verses such as 1 John 2:2 and 4:14 teach that Christ's death was sufficient to cover the sins of every person in the human race. Nevertheless, as John 3:16 and 5:24 reveal, this salvation must be received by personal faith in Christ in order to be appropriated by each individual. Christ has done all that was necessary to satisfy the wrath of God, but each person is responsible for accepting the gift that He has offered.

Making It Personal

21. How should your life change in light of the truth that sin destroys your fellowship with God?

22. What might be some indicators that a believer is denying his sin?

23. Write a prayer both praising God for His provision of Christ as the Advocate in Heaven, and committing to take sin seriously.

24. Memorize 1 John 2:2.

Walking in Obedience and Love

Genuine Christians obey God's Word and love God's people.

1 John 2:3–11

"He that saith he abideth in him ought himself also so to walk, even as he walked" (1 John 2:6).

The United States government goes to great lengths to make U.S. currency hard to counterfeit. They are so successful at making money hard to copy that less than one hundredth of one percent of the currency in circulation is counterfeit.

The government learned its lesson the hard way. At the end of the Civil War, a large portion, between one-third and one-half, of all U.S. paper currency in circulation was fake. The Secret Service was formed in 1865 under the U.S. Treasury Department to counteract the problem. The Secret Service retains that function today, but the frontline of detection is and always has been store clerks. They must authenticate the money before accepting it.

Getting Started

1. Have you ever received counterfeit money? If so, what were the circumstances?

2. How well do you think you would do at determining the authenticity of a piece of paper currency?

In the passage for this study John introduced two of the three marks of an authentic believer. These marks of authenticity are the expected results of God's Spirit at work in the hearts of believers.

Searching the Scriptures

Many people claim they are Christians, but is saying that you are a Christian the same as being one? John defined two marks of the Christian which reveal that a person has truly been saved.

The Mark of Obedience

The first mark of true Christians is obedience to God's Word. Obeying Scripture demonstrates a personal relationship with God. How a person lives reveals whom he loves. The false teachers claimed to know God, but their disobedient lifestyle proved otherwise.

3. What did Jesus tell His disciples, as recorded in John 14:15?

John spoke in terms of a general lifestyle. He had already taught in 1 John 1 that when Christians sin, they need to confess their sins to God to receive forgiveness and cleansing. When John wrote about keeping God's commandments, he did not mean sinless perfection, but the overall pattern of obedience that should characterize a true Christian.

John expanded the criterion of obedience by a set of contrasts (1 John 2:4, 5).

4. Read 1 John 2:4. Why might a person lie about having a personal relationship with God?

Verse 4 presents the negative side of the issue. Some people in John's day said they were Christians even though they had never truly come to know Christ. No doubt some of them were self-deceived, sincerely believing that they knew God when they did not.

5. What factors could play into this type of self-deception?

John urged his readers to probe beyond such claims, for words are tested by works. What a person does is a more accurate indicator than what he declares. Profession without practice is a lie.

John did not say that someone gets to know God by obeying His commandments. Rather, he said that personal knowledge of God leads to obedience. No pattern of obedience is proof that there is no genuine personal knowledge of God.

Verse 5 presents the positive side. Here John viewed the person who keeps the Word of God. Again, John was not suggesting sinless perfection, but a regular, consistent pattern of obedience to God's commandments. This practice of obedience reveals that God's love is at work in a believer's life. People naturally desire to live as they please, resisting submission to God's authority. Only God's presence within a person can produce consistent obedience.

6. How do Galatians 5:22 and 23 expand on the concept that only God's presence within a person can produce consistent obedience?

The set of contrasts (1 John 2:4, 5) determines whether a person truly knows God. Many will claim that they know God. But genuine Christians are marked by a pattern of obedience to Scripture. They want to know God's will. They will submit to His authority. Their obedience reveals that they truly value God, Whom they have come to know.

Revealing Standards

7. What are some standards that people live by today?

8. What standard should believers live by?

Whether or not they consciously recognize it, all people live according to some kind of standard that reflects what they truly love and value. Some people live solely by their own desires. Their self-centeredness reveals that they love themselves more than anyone else. Other people want to please and impress those who are important to them. Their efforts to keep up with others, or to be like them, reveal how much they value what others think.

Christians have a better standard for life. John said that those who claim to know Christ should walk as He walked. They should not do as they please, or act to please their peers, but should walk according to Christ's example.

9. What are some practical ways to learn to walk according to Christ's example?

John 15:1–17 records Jesus' teaching about consistent obedience. He spoke in terms of abiding in Him. Obedience is an obligation for all who know Christ. The person who is abiding in Christ produces obedience.

John spoke in clear-cut categories of obedience and disobedience. The obedient person is a genuine Christian, and the disobedient person does not know God.

By contrast, in 1 Corinthians 3:3 Paul criticized the Corinthian church because some of the Christians were carnal. They should have been living obedient lives, but instead their lives were dominated by sinful actions and attitudes. Paul said that they gave every appearance of being unsaved people.

John and Paul were not contradicting each other, but they were looking at two different but related issues. John's distinction between the obedient and the disobedient was an accurate measure in general terms. Paul, however, added that some Christians slip into a lifestyle inappropriate for their identity.

Too many Christians are guilty of carnality. Carnality is not an acceptable manner of life for Christians and must be confessed and forsaken.

10. Carnality is a mindset or way of thinking. How would you describe the carnal mindset?

The Mark of Love for Others

John moved from the mark of obedience to the second distinguishing mark of Christians, love for others. Living in the light means loving one another.

It is evident that John regarded his readers as true Christians, for he addressed them as brethren. He reassured them that he was not inventing something new. No doubt the false teachers had introduced novel teachings, but John was drawing believers back to the foundational truths of the gospel. Even though John was reminding them of an old commandment, in another sense, it could be called a new commandment, as Jesus Himself described it when He gave it to His disciples.

11. Read John 13:34 and 35. What did Christ say would be the result of His disciples' love for one another?

Christians often speak of having a personal relationship with Christ. That is certainly true and necessary, but there is more to the Christian life. God has also placed them in a community of believers. Loving and obeying God is not just a matter of personal piety; it has a broader social dimension.

12. Evaluate this statement: Building my personal relationship with God is too important for me to waste time with other people.

John pictured the gospel of Christ as a light penetrating the darkness of sin. Christians live in a world in which there is both spiritual light and spiritual darkness. As Christians live out God's truth and love, the true light shines increasingly. Christ's commandment to love one another is part of His strategy to counter the sin and hatred that submerge the world in spiritual darkness.

Measure for Love

Love is a fuzzy concept in today's world. With His command to love, Jesus gave a clear measure for love. He told His disciples to love one another as He had loved them. Christians must not just love as others have loved them. Neither should they settle for loving as they want to be loved. Instead, they must love as Christ has already loved them. Only God's indwelling Spirit can produce that quality of love in a person. That is why true love for one another is an accurate mark of the genuine Christian.

13. What is kindness?

14. What characterizes love that is pleasing to the Lord?

15. Why is it easier to show simple kindness to our Christian brothers and sisters rather than real love?

In 1 John 2:9 and 10, John once again used a set of contrasts to clarify the difference between those who falsely claim to be Christians and those who are genuine followers of Christ. It is not sufficient to listen to what a person claims; the proof is in the loving.

16. Put 1 John 2:9 into your own words.

In verse 9 John considered the case of a person who claims to be in the light. According to 1 John, being in the light means living in the realm of God, or living in the way God approves. Even though an individual may claim to be in the light, in practice he may hate his brother. "Hate" here speaks of the absence of love. It is not necessarily active hostility, but it is the failure to love as Christ commanded.

John concluded that the lack of love indicates that such a person is living in the realm of darkness. Jesus told His disciples that all people would know they were His disciples by the love they displayed for one another (John 13:35). The test of being in the light is love for others. In fact, as 1 John 4:20 and 21 teach, loving God and loving others are two sides of the same coin. The mark of love insists that social relationships are an accurate measure of spiritual reality.

First John 2:10 is the positive counterpart to the previous verse. The person who loves his brother is the one who is abiding in the light. God's Spirit is working in his heart, producing love for others.

John went on to add, "There is none occasion of stumbling in him." The person who is walking in God's light has his values aligned properly. He loves what God loves, so he does what God desires. Instead of following his own selfish impulses into sin, the person living in the light denies himself in order to serve God's cause. Living for God means loving others, and loving others keeps one from stumbling into sin.

17. How would loving others keep you from stumbling into sin in your home? in your church?

Necessary Social Dimension

John concluded this passage about the mark of love with strong words. He rejected the idea that a person's relationship with God is a private matter between the individual and God. He insisted that genuine Christianity has a necessary social dimension.

This is not social gospel theology that say that one gets saved through loving others. Rather, John taught that when a person truly loves God he will also love others.

18. How did your love for others change after you trusted Christ as your Savior?

John concluded that the person who hates his brother is in darkness and walks in darkness (2:11). Once again, he used hatred to cover all forms of unloving behavior. To John's thinking, indifference and careless disregard of others are passive forms of hatred. By refusing to love actively, a person is in reality hurting others.

19. What are some ways Christians show indifference or careless disregard to each other?

20. How can a Christian with a right understanding of love show it to others?

Active or passive hatred of others leads to all sorts of spiritual calamities. Because hatred is sin, it leads to spiritual blindness. Those who are spiritually blind cannot see others accurately, so they become unable to perceive and respond to their needs. Their blindness leads them into ethical aimlessness, because they have no moral compass by which to direct their lives.

The Bible teaches that God loved the world. That is the kind of love God produces in His people.

Making It Personal

21. To whom have you shown indifference instead of love?

22. Ask God how He wants you to love those you have failed to love.

23. At its core, love involves service. To whom should you reach out and serve with God's sacrificial love today?

24. Memorize 1 John 2:6.

Lesson 5

Look Before You Love

All Christians need to be careful to love God,
not the world.

1 John 2:12–17

"The world passeth away, and the lust thereof:
but he that doeth the will of God abideth for
ever" (1 John 2:17).

But WAIT! Not only do you get one set of ninety-six kitchen knives, but you also get a second set for free! And we'll even throw in this pair of kitchen shears if you call in the next thirty minutes. You get all this, a $400.00 value, for two easy payments of $19.95 each!"

Ever get pulled into an infomercial that sounds a lot like this? Most people find themselves mesmerized at one time or another by such presentations. Some even give in and buy the 192 knives just to get the shears for free!

Getting Started

1. When has a marketing appeal caught your attention to the point that you decided to buy the product?

2. What did you think of the product once you got it?

The apostle John talked about marketing schemes in the spiritual realm. He gave instructions to his readers about resisting those schemes and focusing love on God instead.

Searching the Scriptures

In 1 John 2:3–11, John presented the first two marks of genuine Christians: obedience and love. He developed the third mark, truth, in 2:18–27. Before he spoke of truth, however, John had some important words of challenge for his readers.

First Addresses

In 1 John 2:12–14, John addressed his readers with three expressions: little children, fathers, and young men. Many view these terms as three developmental categories. In spiritual experience, some of the readers were little children, or young believers. Others were mature believers, the fathers of the church; and others were the young men, the backbone of the ministry, those who shouldered a major part of the work.

3. Is it wrong to aspire to a place of respected spiritual maturity? Explain.

There is another possible interpretation. Several times John called the whole group little children. Since John did not mention the three stages in chronological order, some have concluded that he used all three terms to refer to all of the readers from different angles. They all were spiritual children of God, had all achieved a measure of spiritual maturity, and, in light of the threat from false teachers, all needed to respond as courageous young men.

4. Why is courage needed in the Christian life?

In all John gave six reasons for writing to his readers.

5. Read 1 John 2:12–14. Record what John wrote about his readers' spiritual state.

In his first statement to little children, John stated that he was writing to them because their sins were forgiven. The recipients of 1 John were children of God because they had received Christ as their Savior and therefore forgiveness of sin. John did not doubt the genuineness of their salvation.

John wrote to the "fathers," because walking with God over a period of years had brought them into a deep understanding of Him (2:13). Their relationship with God had begun with forgiveness of sins, but it had grown into an intimate knowledge of Him.

John addressed the "young men" because they had overcome the wicked one. The Devil is at the root of all evil, including false teaching (3:8). As the believers faced the threat of error, they were fighting against the formidable foe of Satan. But, through faith in God, they experienced the reality that "greater is he that is in you, than he that is in the world" (4:4).

Second Addresses

John proceeded to address each of the groups again. In speaking to the little children, he reminded them that they had come to know the Father, just as the fathers had done. To the fathers, John restated his reason in verse 13, that is, because they had known Him Who is from the beginning. Finally, to the young men John added some important words. They were able to overcome the wicked one because they drew their strength from the Word of God abiding in them (2:14). Their spiritual strength in the face of conflict came from their comprehensive commitment to Scripture. They had learned the Bible well, which equipped them to live courageously for God.

When spiritual challenges arise, it is easy for Christians to doubt God and their own faith. John reminded believers of Who Christ is: the Son of God, Who came to earth as a man and died as a substitutionary sacrifice. Then John rebuilt their confidence that they were indeed children of God who could stand in His strength against the enemy's onslaught.

Ungodly Values

In 2:15–17 John looked at the worldview that underlies the error his readers faced. That worldview included a counterfeit system of values, which John called "the world."

6. According to Matthew 4:8 and 9 and 2 Corinthians 4:4, what is Satan's relationship to this world system?

God created humans with the capacity for love. The question is not, Will we love? but What will we love? Spiritual problems emerge when people choose to love the world's values rather than giving their hearts fully to God.

John commanded his readers: "Love not the world, neither the things that are in the world." The key to understanding this command is to determine how John meant the term "world." In the New Testament, this word can refer to the universe, the planet, the sum total of people on the earth (cf. John 3:16), or unsaved people. When John commanded his readers not to love the world, he did not mean any of these. Rather, "world" here refers to a system of values that is opposed to God and that characterizes those who reject Him.

7. What are "values"?

8. How are a person's values revealed?

9. What are some of the values specifically held by the world?

In Jesus' prayer for His people in John 17, He spoke of the relationship of Christians to the world.

10. According to John 17:13–19, what do Christians in the world need?

On the one hand, Christians do not belong to the world in the sense that they do not share its values and priorities (John 17:14). Because of this, the world hates and rejects those who are committed to Christ. Just as Jesus was not of the world in the sense of holding its values, His people are not of the world (17:16).

On the other hand, the Father does not remove Christians from the world. Jesus prayed that the Father would guard them from the attacks of the evil one (17:15). So, Christians have to expect conflict because they live in enemy territory.

While the world is where Christians live, it should not be what Christians love. As John stated clearly in 1 John 2:15, love for the world robs a person's capacity for loving God.

11. Why does loving the world affect our ability to love God?

Truly loving God demands we give Him all our love. God doesn't want part of our hearts.

12. What are some practical ways that we can cultivate love for God?

The Bible often uses the metaphor of adultery to picture those who transfer their devotion away from God to other things (James 4:4). Worldliness is primarily a matter of the heart, because at its root it loves the world instead of God. Godliness is active, wholehearted devotion to God, which comes from setting one's heart on Him.

Three Categories of Worldliness

Some Christians have established lists of actions to define worldliness. It's true that certain activities are out of bounds for those who truly love God. But John did not set forth a list of what to do and what not to do. Instead, he grouped all that is in the world into three broad categories (2:16). Each of these categories is a basic attitude that produces a wide variety of activities. John's threefold description of worldliness covers all cultures and time periods. It probes our hearts, desires, motives, and ambitions. These are the attitudes that have tripped up countless people, from Adam and Eve to the present day.

"Lust of the flesh" refers to desires derived from the sinful human nature. The Bible teaches that the heart is deceitful above all things and desperately wicked (Jeremiah 17:9). In Galatians 5:19–21 Paul listed a sobering assortment of sinful actions and attitudes that he called the "works of the flesh." This sinful behavior comes naturally to humans because of their inherited sin nature. Loving the world, then, includes doing what comes naturally to sinners, rather than living by the Spirit.

13. Given our natural tendency to sin, how successful will a believer be if he just tries harder to resist sinning? Whose help does he need? (See Ephesians 5:18.)

"Lust of the eyes" is a response to temptations from outside. The eyes are attracted to things in the environment that prompt them to desire what is contrary to God's will. This category of sin focuses on external appearances rather than spiritual insight. It can easily lead to materialism, because it values what it sees more than what God says.

14. Evaluate this statement: I don't worry about what I watch on TV, because I'm mature enough to handle sinful influences.

"Pride of life" speaks of a desire to look better than others. "Pride" in this context refers to boastful arrogance. Instead of being satisfied with what is good, it insists on being better than someone else. Instead of being content with what is lovely, it craves being lovelier than others. It is satisfied only when it can boast about being the best. Rather than cultivating humble dependence upon God, it exalts self at the expense of others. It is a self-centered devotion to ambition, prestige, and influence that leads away from devotion to God.

Consequences of Choices

When people love the wrong person or the wrong things, they typically end up with long-term regrets, pain, and scars. So John urged his readers to consider the consequences of their choices. In verse 17 he contrasted what love for the world produces with what love for God produces.

15. According to 1 John 2:17, what is the contrast between what love for the world produces and what love for God produces?

The world is compelling in its appeal, because it seems to offer immediate gratification of our desires. The world appears to satisfy the desires of the flesh, the desires of the eyes, and the desires people have to look better than others. All of these are powerful inducements to love the world.

16. How can Christians operate in the world without becoming worldly?

As a system, the world is passing away. Consequently, loving the world is like boarding a sinking ship. It has no future, but obeying the will of God leads to lasting life. The wise person looks beyond the appearance of immediate pleasure to the reality of eternal blessing. He invests his life in doing God's will, because that alone will stand the test of time.

17. Why do people often choose to love the world? Why do people hesitate to do the will of God?

Christians today face the same basic choice that John's original readers did: Whom or what will we love? If we choose to love the world, we will eventually find that we have chosen disappointment, for loving the world has no future. If, however, we choose to love God by doing His will, we will find the path to true and lasting fulfillment.

Making It Personal

18. When you give into the lust of the flesh, the lust of the eyes, or the pride of life how satisfied are you ultimately with your decision?

19. Why do you suppose we give into the same sins that we have already learned are hurtful and destructive?

20. What key steps might you need to take to live by the Spirit, follow spiritual insight, and center on God?

21. Memorize 1 John 2:17.

The Test of Truth

Genuine Christians accept as truth that Jesus is the Son of God.

1 John 2:18–27

"But the anointing which ye have received of him abideth in you, and ye need not that any man teach you: but as the same anointing teacheth you of all things, and is truth, and is no lie, and even as it hath taught you, ye shall abide in him" (1 John 2:27).

The website EarnMyDegree.com offers an article titled "How to Avoid Fake Diplomas and Degree Scams," which provides seven signs that an online degree program is a scam:

1. It promises a degree in no time.
2. You can't contact anyone about the program.
3. Online forums and blogs have bad things to say about it.
4. Government education agencies have never heard of the program.
5. The site talks about getting your degree, but not the education part.
6. It sounds too good to be true.
7. The school isn't accredited.

So, anyone looking for an online school can learn the truth about online education and, therefore, how to detect lies about it. But there's no website that can teach a person how to detect spiritual lies. The only way to do that is to know the truth. And that requires knowledge of the Bible.

Getting Started

1. How well do you need to know the Bible before you can detect spiritual lies?

2. Do you believe you are currently at that point? What do you need to do to be better prepared?

Searching the Scriptures

Third Mark of a True Christian

In 1 John 2:18–27 John made a clear distinction between his readers and those who were trying to seduce them by false teaching. First he spoke about the error of the antichristian opponents. Then he contrasted them with the Christians who possessed true spiritual knowledge.

Because sin is deceitful, it is crucial for Christians to be discerning. Young children can get into problems because they are unaware of dangers. As John addressed his "little children" in the faith, he wanted to put them on their guard against errors that could lead them into spiritual defeat. As John had just written, it was necessary that the Christians demonstrate love in their lives. Undiscerning love, however, could be disastrous. Love must be bounded by truth.

3. Why can undiscerning love be disastrous?

Shortly before His death, Jesus warned His disciples that false christs and false teachers would arise (Mark 13:21, 22). Similar warnings were also uttered by Jude (Jude 18). When John wrote at the end of the first century, the false teachers were already beginning their attack on the truth.

4. How might you identify a false teacher?

No doubt John's readers understood about the Antichrist who will emerge during the tribulation period. They might have been tempted to think that figure was a threat only for some remote future time. So John turned their attention to the immediate issue: They were living in "the last time," a time of grave spiritual danger. If they did not recognize the problem, the results could be devastating.

5. How will a proper sense of urgency show itself in the life of a Christian?

The future Antichrist of the Tribulation will be the culmination of a succession of antichrists throughout history. John described them as antichrists because they deny that Jesus is indeed the Messiah (2:22). They oppose Jesus Christ by denying His true nature (4:3). Through their error, they lead the charge of Satan's forces mobilized against God and His people.

6. Why is it important to understand the false views of Christ's Person that have been presented throughout church history?

Sadly, the false teachers were people who had once identified themselves as Christians. Their names may have been on the church roll, but they were never included in God's Book of Life. They had given the appearance of being Christians, but in reality they were not true believers. In fact, the false teachers had presented themselves as though they belonged to the band of the apostles, but they were actually frauds. By their defection from Christ, they showed their true colors as antichrists.

If love is not bounded by truth, Christians can easily be deceived by false teachers whose smooth words mask their denial of Christ. John's warning against the error of the antichrists in the first century is equally relevant in the twenty-first century.

7. According to 1 John 2:20 and 21, why were the true believers able to know the truth?

The New Testament teaches that the Holy Spirit comes to indwell all genuine Christians. The fact of the Spirit's presence is conclusive proof that a person has truly been born again as God's child. As part of His ministry, the Spirit guides the believer into true spiritual knowledge (cf. 1 Corinthians 2; 3).

8. What is the Holy Spirit's primary means of guiding us into knowledge?

The final phrase in 1 John 2:20 contains a difficult textual problem. One reading, translated "ye know all things," emphasizes that the Holy Spirit is the source of all true knowledge. The false teachers of John's day likely claimed to possess special knowledge. John countered their claims by saying that the Holy Spirit provides knowledge of all things.

The other reading is translated "you all know." Here the emphasis is on the fact that the Christians to whom John wrote, not the false teachers, were the ones who had genuine knowledge.

Both readings are consistent with other passages in the New Testament which declare that the Holy Spirit teaches all Christians God's truth and that His teaching encompasses even "the deep things of God" (1 Corinthians 2:10). However, verse 21 fits especially well with the reading "you all know." John reassured his readers by regarding them as genuine Christians who knew the truth. He was not correcting them, but he was confirming their spiritual status as true Christians. Their knowledge of the truth was proof that the Holy Spirit was indwelling them, because His teaching ministry was active in their lives. This clearly distinguished them from the erroneous antichrists, who did not know truth.

9. How is the Spirit's teaching ministry active in your life? What can you now understand that you couldn't before you received Christ?

View of the Son

10. What are the fundamental truths about Jesus Christ revealed in God's Word?

The central truth of Christianity is the person of Christ. According to the Bible, He is the Son of God, Who took on human flesh when He came to earth (John 1:1–14). Identifying in this way with the human race, He died on the cross as the only perfect substitute for sinners. If Jesus was not divine, His death on the cross could not have satisfied God's righteous demands.

The deity of Jesus Christ is nonnegotiable. It is impossible to be wrong about the Person of Christ and still hold to the truth. As John put it in verse 22, those who deny Jesus Christ, the Son of God, also deny God the Father.

11. Read 1 John 2:22 and 23. Why do you think John went so far as to call the false teachers liars and antichrists?

Many people want to accept Jesus as a good man, a moral teacher, and a worthy example, but not as the Son of God. This is not adequate. The only logical alternatives are to view Jesus either as both God and good, or as a lying, fraudulent imposter.

John continued in verse 23 to state that belief in Christ and belief in God the Father are necessarily linked together. Jesus said clearly in John 14:6 that He is the only way to the Father.

12. Why is it impossible to affirm the Father if you deny Christ?

Accepting Jesus as the Son of God brings a person into fellowship with the Father. John's readers had come to know God through placing their faith in Christ. The false teachers had rejected Christ, and in so doing had rejected the Father.

Commitment to God's Word

13. According to 1 John 2:24–27, what would be these believers' defense against the antichrists' teaching?

John challenged believers to abide in the truth that they had learned from the beginning of their Christian experience. As John had already stated several times in the letter, they needed to hold to the truth that they had known "from the beginning" rather than becoming enamored with the new teachings that moved away from the truth of the gospel.

14. Why might the readers have found the new teachings attractive?

John was most concerned that the Christians maintain a continuing commitment to the truth. The English words "abide," "remain," and "continue" all translate the same Greek verb. By this repetition, John emphasized that commitment to God's revealed truth is integrally connected to commitment to God Himself. Staying with God's Word will keep believers staying with the Son and with the Father. In a parallel way, leaving God's Word destroys fellowship with God.

In the first century, like today, there were people whose ears itched for something new and different to believe (cf. 2 Timothy 4:3). John insisted that God's truth does not change, so commitment to His Word must not change. Any change from the truth is a detour into error.

15. What should we do when presented with spiritual teachings that we are unfamiliar with?

Abiding in the truth also gives Christians great hope for the future. In His Word, God has provided the promise of eternal life, which is found only through belief in Jesus Christ, the Son of God. The familiar words of John 3:16 demonstrate that whoever believes in the Son has everlasting life. John 3:36 presents both sides of the issue: "He that believeth on the Son hath everlasting life: and he that believeth not the Son shall not see life; but the wrath of God abideth on him."

John had disclosed the threat and described its dangers. It was up to the readers, however, to act on the warning that they had received. Now that they knew the facts of the matter, they must not let the false teachers deceive and seduce them.

The best defense against error is abiding in the truth. The Holy Spirit is the internal witness to God's truth (2:27). He is an unerring guide to keep God's people from error. Additionally, the Bible is God's unchanging truth in written form. To be protected from error, Christians need to walk in the Spirit and stay in the Bible. Those who stay with God's truth do not slip into error, because truth enables them to see error for the fraud that it is.

16. What are some practical ways to abide in the truth?

God does not promise that His people will be immune from temptation. Indeed, they will have to confront error of all sorts. What God does promise is that He will provide what His people need to overcome the temptation successfully. With the Holy Spirit in their hearts and with the Bible in their minds, Christians are equipped to see through the seductions of error and stand courageously for truth.

Making It Personal

17. What should you include in your message as you share Christ?

Some false religions, such as Mormonism, emphasize good character and family values. Their followers are generally nice people with admirable dedication. Often such false religions will attract believers based on these qualities. A believer who is abiding in the truth will never succumb to the seductiveness of false religions.

18. What are you doing to abide in the truth?

19. What can you do to prepare yourself better to stand against the seductiveness of false teachers?

20. Memorize 1 John 2:27.

When He Shall Appear

*Christ's coming should produce confidence
and commitment.*

1 John 2:28—3:3

**"Beloved, now are we the sons of God, and it
doth not yet appear what we shall be: but we
know that, when he shall appear, we shall be
like him; for we shall see him as he is" (1 John
3:2).**

February 7, 2011, was a bitterly cold, snowy day in Clarksville, Tennessee. It was also the day 189 sons/brothers/ fathers returned home from a year in Afghanistan. Their families did not wait in the warm comfort of a hanger, but out on the tarmac, where they huddled together attempting to stay warm. When they heard the sound of the plane carrying their loved ones, they cheered. The cheer grew louder when the aircraft materialized through a white sheet of snow. Their men were home.

The families were ushered back indoors, where the soldiers joined them for their much-anticipated reunions. An observer wrote: "How families reacted to their reunion differed wildly. Some kissed, while others stood in the middle of the tumult lost in each other's company. Some posed for pictures." After fifteen minutes, the two groups separated: the soldiers to load buses, the families back to their lives, until time for more private reunions.

Getting Started

1. When have you waited for someone with great expectation? What were some of your feelings at that time? How did your experience affect your behavior?

2. How can we apply those experiences to waiting for Christ's return?

Searching the Scriptures

Confident Waiting

3. Read 1 John 2:28. When did you last think seriously about Christ's return?

John challenged believers to abide in Christ (1 John 2:28). Knowing the truth is not enough; knowledge must be matched by obedience. To motivate them to continue in Christ, John turned their attention to the future, when Christ will appear again. When Christ returns, those who have continued in obedience to Him will greet Him in confidence.

4. Sometimes people pretend to obey God so they look good to other Christians. How will they respond when Christ returns?

One thing is certain: all believers will have to appear before Christ when He comes. Those who have honored and obeyed Him will appear in confidence. Those who have not honored and obeyed Him will shrink away in shame. Each person's response to the appearance of Christ will reflect how he has respected or disrespected the truth about Christ.

5. According to Romans 14:10–12 and 2 Corinthians 5:10 and 11, where will believers appear before Christ?

6. What two words come to your mind when you contemplate giving an account of your life before Christ?

Righteousness and the True Believer

First John 2:28 states that a person's view of Christ affects his view of Christ's return. Verse 29 develops that general point more specifically. Essential to right belief about Christ is righteous behavior by Christians. It is important to know the truth, but it is equally essential that a believer practices the truth. In other words, good theology must be matched by godly living.

First John 1:9 says that Christ is "faithful and just to forgive us our sins, and to cleanse us from all unrighteousness." Verse 29 of chapter 2 speaks of knowing that Christ is "righteous." The word for "righteous" is the same as the word for "just" in 1:9. Christ is righteous because He embodies the perfect standard of divine holiness. There is no hint of error or flaw in Christ. He is nothing short of absolute perfection as the Son of God. The righteousness of Christ was the very point at which the false teachers in John's day failed to honor Christ as He deserved.

7. Read 1 John 2:29. How do you react to having Christ as your standard for life? Are you frustrated, humbled, motivated?

The last half of verse 29 could be translated, "You know that everyone who does righteousness has been begotten by Him." Righteous acts do not produce or merit a relationship with God, but spiritual birth through Christ produces righteous living. What a person is in Christ (saved) should control how that person behaves (living righteously).

God Himself is righteous, and He wants those who are born into His family to evidence righteousness. They cannot do this in their own strength, but through the Holy Spirit, God has provided all of the spiritual resources they need. At the same time, each Christian is responsible to use those spiritual resources by living faithfully according to God's standards.

8. How would having an artistic guide with you in trying to copy a painting be like having the Holy Spirit with you to help you live like Christ?

For God's children, obedience is an obligation that requires full commitment. John challenged his readers to live up to what they were in Christ. Those who are truly born of God need to look and live like their Heavenly Father by doing as He commands.

God's Love

John's focus on his readers as God's children continued into chapter 3. Being born into God's family is a privilege rooted in God's indescribable love.

9. Read 1 John 3:1. Why might believers be prone to take God's love for granted?

For Christians to truly value their position in Christ, they need to comprehend how they received that status. It did not come from their efforts or their own righteous deeds. The Bible teaches that all have sinned and fallen short of the glory of God (Romans 3:23). All humans are like sheep that have gone astray by turning to their own way (Isaiah 53:6). Nevertheless, God demonstrated His love for unworthy sinners by giving His own Son, Jesus Christ, to die for all sinners (Romans 5:8).

The term "what manner" in 1 John 3:1 refers to a high quality or a vast quantity. The love of God goes beyond description. What the world calls love is cheap costume jewelry compared to the pure gold of God's pure love.

In His love, God the Father took the initiative to reach out to undeserving people. Later, in 4:10, John says, "Herein is love, not that we loved God, but that He loved us, and sent his Son to be the propitiation for our sins." The measure of love is what one is willing to sacrifice for the person loved. God's love was so great that He gave His only Son to die for sinners (John 3:16).

God's love did not stop with forgiveness, as great as that is. His love continued to take those undeserving sinners and welcome them into His family.

10. Finish this statement: To me, being a child of God means . . .

Christians have a relationship with God, their Heavenly Father. They can look forward to enjoying eternity in His home in Heaven.

11. According to 1 John 3:1, what is the result of being in God's family?

12. What does that mean?

There is a down side to being God's child. When Christ lived on earth, even His own nation did not receive Him. Although some accepted His claims, most refused to believe in Him. The world as a whole did not know Him, understand Him, or appreciate Him. Instead, they rejected and executed the Son of God. The world does not appreciate and value God's children any more than it appreciated and valued Christ. In fact, the more a person fellowships with God, the less the world can understand him.

Rejection is always difficult to accept. John's readers had a painful choice to make. On the one hand, they could find human acceptance in the world, but at the price of abandoning their love for the Father (2:15). On the other hand, they could love their Father by faithful obedience to His Word, but that would bring criticism and ridicule by the false teachers.

The choice they faced is the same kind of choice that confronts Christians today. They cannot be at home in both God's family and the world. They must choose what they will value, who they will love, and how they will live. By pointing to what God has done in the past in bestowing His undeserved love, John challenged Christians to hold fast to their position as the children of God and to resist all temptations to yield to the world.

God's Plan

In verse 2 John shifted his attention from what God has done in the past to what He will do in the future. All those who have accepted Christ by faith have become members of God's family.

This was a wonderful truth for John's original readers and for all Christians in every age. That, however, is not the end of the story. Just as human parents have great plans for their children, so God the Father is planning and working to bring His children to their full potential. As John went on to say in verse 2, for Christians the best is yet to come.

13. Read 1 John 3:2. What exciting truth did John reveal about the believer's future?

14. What do you think will be the most exciting part of that reality?

In 2:28 John mentioned the future appearing of Christ as the motivation for obedience. In 3:2 John used the same phrase, "when he shall appear," to provide the basis for hope. Not only will Christians see Christ again when He returns, but when they see Him, they will become like Him.

People often think of salvation in terms of deliverance from the penalty of sin and death. That certainly is crucial, but salvation includes much more. The New Testament teaches that the ultimate result of salvation is glorification (cf. Romans 8:30). By His gracious work, God will transform the lives of His children so they become like Christ. That glorification will be accomplished when Christ appears again.

15. In what ways will believers become like Christ?

God the Father wants to bring His children to their full potential so they truly bear the family resemblance. Looking at Christians today, it is all too evident that they are still far from what God will make them to be. In fact, God's finished product will be beyond anything that presently can be seen or imagined. Christians now are like a sketch. When Christ appears, God will fill in the colors and the details of His masterpiece of glorification.

Even though all God will do lies beyond present understanding, He has given to believers an important hint. John said, "We shall be like him; for we shall see him as he is." When believers see Christ, they will be transformed to be like Him by the Father's gracious work. It will be truly amazing to see what God has done with sinners whom He saved by grace.

A Present Purity

Those who have been born again into God's family should have a changed lifestyle. God's love, which brought unworthy sinners into His family, should stimulate them to pure living, as should the future hope of glorification. Those who have their hope set on Christ's appearing should commit themselves to lives patterned after Him. God the Father is working to produce Christlikeness in each of His children. Each Christian needs to cooperate with what God is working to accomplish.

16. How do Christians cooperate with God's working in them?

17. What are some ways that believers may not cooperate with God's working?

For Christians, Jesus Christ is the fixed standard for life. Those who keep their eyes focused on Him will learn to live as He desires. More and more they will look like Him in their behavior.

Making It Personal

18. How can you be prepared for Christ's coming?

19. How will you respond to the certainty of Christ's coming?

20. What can you do now to continue/start the process of becoming more like Christ?

21. Are you ready if He returns today?

22. Memorize 1 John 3:2.

What Christ Came to Do

A true believer's behavior will match his or her belief.

1 John 3:4–10

"In this the children of God are manifest, and the children of the devil: whosoever doeth not righteousness is not of God, neither he that loveth not his brother" (1 John 3:10).

I n 2007 a self-proclaimed environmentalist famous for his views on global warming was highly criticized for having a home in Nashville that used twelve times the amount of energy than that used by average homes in the same area. This behavior seemed inconsistent with his stated beliefs, and his political enemies jumped on it. They circulated an e-mail comparing his home to the home of a political rival. What wasn't as well circulated was a later report on how he "completed a host of improvements to make the home more energy efficient" or that "a building-industry group has praised the house as one of the nation's most environmentally friendly." Apparently what the man believes about the environment did affect his behavior eventually.

Getting Started

1. How does what you believe about *sin* affect *your* behavior?

2. Is there a difference between what believers *know* about sin and what believers *believe* about sin? Explain.

Searching the Scriptures

When Christ came the first time to die for sin, He opened the way for righteous living for His people. In two parallel sections (1 John 3:4–7 and 3:8–10), John built a bridge between right belief in Christ and righteous behavior in Christians.

Sin Is . . .

3. Read 1 John 3:4. Using your own words, describe sin.

The Bible states clearly that all have sinned, failing to reach God's glory (Romans 3:23). But sin is a subject humans find hard to accept. To make the situation less convicting, people concede that they make mistakes, have weaknesses, or use bad judgment. Even when they use the term "sin" they often intend some diluted version of the concept.

4. Why are people willing to admit mistakes, but not sins?

In 1 John 3:4 John defined sin in unmistakable terms. He said that whoever sins is in reality doing what is lawless. Sin is not an excusable human lapse. It is a serious act of rebellion against God. The psalmist, confessing his sin, stated: "Against thee, thee only, have I sinned, and done this evil in thy sight" (Psalm 51:4). He was not denying that he had sinned against other people and wronged them terribly. Rather, he was acknowledging that at its deepest level his sin was rebellion against God's law.

The essence of sin is lawlessness. It is a refusal to live under God's authority, so it acts in opposition to God's will. Instead of humbly obeying God's law, the sinner exalts himself above God and tries to become a law unto himself.

5. When have you observed people becoming a law unto themselves?

Throughout the New Testament, false teachers resisted God's law as proclaimed by Jesus and the apostles. In rejecting truth, they promoted error. Their refusal to live by God's Word caused them to develop beliefs and behaviors that violated it. By setting up their own standards contrary to God, they became lawless sinners and encouraged others to follow them into lawlessness.

Sinless Pattern of Life

When Christ came to earth, He came to take away sins. He paid the ultimate price, the pain and humiliation of the cross, to defeat sin. Since Christ died to eliminate sin, it makes no sense for Christians to embrace sin. Christians should not harbor, encourage, or excuse sin. Christ's death demonstrated that living in Christ and living in sin cannot go together.

6. Why is the truth of the incompatibility of living for Christ and living in sin crucial to include in the discipleship process?

First John 3:6 applies the theology of Christ to the practice of Christians: "Whosoever abideth in him sinneth not." This statement does not speak of sinless perfection. Rather, it describes the consistent lifestyle of true Christians. It could be paraphrased, "Everyone who abides in Christ does not have a pattern of sin in his life." Abiding in Christ is living in fellowship with Him (John 15:5). Consistent sin is a mark of those who do not know Christ, but Christians should bear the marks of their position in Christ. In other words, knowing Christ should radically change a believer's lifestyle.

Because Christ and sin are incompatible, those who abide in Christ should not maintain lives marked by sin. They will sin, but sinning should be followed by confession and cleansing. Sin should not become the typical pattern of life.

Those whose lives reveal a pattern of consistent sin demonstrate that they have not seen or known Christ. Sin is the result of spiritual blindness and ignorance. It is not, as the false teachers claimed, an indication of superior understanding.

John kept pulling his readers back to the Christian life as it should be lived. He began with Christ, and from that he went to how Christians should act and think. This was in contrast to the false teachers. They started with their sinful actions and changed their beliefs to match their behavior.

7. Why must we never begin with our sin and change our beliefs to match?

Standard for Life

The false teachers were attempting to deceive the Christians about sin, so John strongly warned them, "Let no man deceive you" (3:7). Then he set up an unalterable standard for measuring all of life.

8. How can we keep from being spiritually deceived?

Every action, attitude, and motive should be measured by what Christ Himself taught and did. This is the fixed moral standard that applies to all.

9. Which do you tend to consider more: Christ's teachings or His works? Why?

10. How can believers challenge themselves to measure their actions, attitudes, and motives by Christ's teachings and actions?

John taught that righteous conduct is produced by righteous character. Those who have been born into God's family receive the imputed righteousness of Christ. Their position in Christ then shapes their practice. The indwelling Holy Spirit produces the fruit of godly, righteous living. As Christians abide in Christ, they become more like Him in what they do, say, and desire. Their righteous behavior reveals that they indeed belong to Him.

The false teachers were seeking to move them in the opposite direction. Instead of encouraging them in righteousness, they were trying to move them away from Christ. Their erroneous beliefs would inevitably lead to unrighteous behavior. Anything that deviates from Christ is a move away from God's righteous standard.

Children of the Devil

11. Read 1 John 3:8 and John 8:44. Why is it important to know that unbelievers are called children of the Devil?

12. Do you normally think of a "nice" unbeliever as a child of the Devil? Explain.

Just as the Bible speaks of Christians as the children of God, so it describes unbelievers as the children of the Devil. Since his fall, the Devil has always resisted God, broken His law, and undercut His program.

Sinful conduct shows the undeniable mark of Satan's influence. Lives characterized by a pattern of sin belong to Satan's family. For them, sin is a natural response of resistance to God. Like their spiritual father, the Devil, they miss the mark of God's righteousness. By following Satan's lead, they have joined his struggle against God. Instead of living under God's law, they have chosen lawless rebellion.

Christ's Victory

The Devil conspired to destroy the works of God, but Christ came to destroy the works of the Devil. Satan cleverly tempted Adam and Eve, leading them into sin. Since then the Devil has used various wiles and strategies to defeat God's people and tear down God's work. Sometimes he comes as a roaring lion seeking to devour Christians (1 Peter 5:8, 9). Other times he trips Christians up by subtle schemes (2 Corinthians 11:3). Satan seeks every opportunity to undo God's plan.

13. Why might Satan use different strategies in trying to get believers to fall?

Satan seems powerful to us because we find it easy to fall to his temptations. He still works feverishly to subvert God's program, and in the process he damages many lives. Nevertheless, Scripture makes it clear that Satan's days are numbered (Revelation 20). Christ has destroyed his power.

First John 3:9 contains a powerful truth about the position of God's children: they cannot sin because they are born of God. This does not mean Christians are perfect and incapable of any sin, for that would contradict 1 John 1:8–10. Rather, God's children have a radical spiritual dynamic that gives them victory over sin.

Those who belong to the Devil's family commit sin because all humans have been born with a sin nature. Those who have been born again have become new creatures in Christ (cf. 2 Corinthians 5:17). God changes His people from the inside out, making them "partakers of the divine nature" (2 Peter 1:4).

It is true that Christians sin. However, Christians must be careful to interpret their experience in light of Scripture rather than interpreting Scripture in light of their experience.

14. How would you expand on the idea of "interpreting your experience in light of Scripture"?

Just as physical growth is a gradual progress toward the goal of maturity, so Christian growth is a gradual progress toward the goal of Christlikeness. For the Christian who is abiding in Christ, sin becomes less frequent as he learns to live up to his position in Christ. At the same time, the sin nature always leaves Christians open to the possibility of spiritual failure.

15. How does it help to compare Christian growth with physical growth?

Righteousness and Love

John's readers faced the challenge of evaluating religious teachers who claimed to come from God. This epistle was written to give them some distinguishing marks of true Christians. They could use these marks both to evaluate the character of their teachers and to guide them in their own spiritual development.

As John drew this passage to a close in 1 John 3:10, he divided all humans into two families. All people are either children of God or children of the Devil. Just as children typically resemble their physical parents in how they appear, so people resemble their spiritual fathers in how they live. Actions and attitudes reveal a person's spiritual heritage.

Christians who have been born into God's family should live in a distinctively godly way. Throughout this letter John exhorted his readers to live in truth, obedience, and love, because those qualities are appropriate for God's children. Christ came to take away sins and to destroy the works of the Devil, so His people should live transformed lives that reflect what He has done in them. As God's children, Christians should live out the godly life that He has planted within them.

On the other hand, the children of the Devil resemble their spiritual father. Just as the Devil is committed to unrighteousness, so his children do not live by God's righteous standards. Their lives are characterized by disobedience.

16. Why might John have used love for one's brother as major indicator of a true relationship with God (v. 10)?

17. How has your love for others changed as you have grown as a believer?

In addition, the Devil and his children are unwilling and unable to love others. The love of God that flows though the lives of His children to touch others is foreign to Satan and his people. Love is a fruit of the Holy Spirit's activity in the Christian.

Making It Personal

18. How well does your behavior match your beliefs?

19. Would someone conclude you are a believer based on your behavior? Would someone ever tell you that you remind him of Christ? Why or why not?

20. Write a prayer that you might utilize Christ's power and experience spiritual victory in the week ahead.

21. Memorize 1 John 3:10.

Loving in Deed and in Truth

Genuine love is demonstrated by works, not words.

1 John 3:11–24

"Hereby perceive we the love of God, because he laid down his life for us: and we ought to lay down our lives for the brethren" (1 John 3:16).

In June 2010, a twenty-one-year old Florida man admitted to killing his nineteen-year-old brother. It began with a fight between the two. Stanley, the older, strangled his brother and buried him in the side yard of their family home. The men's mother saw Stanley burying something. "It's just some things that belonged to my girlfriend," he explained to her. But the boys' sister insisted that their dad check on what Stanley had buried, and Stanley's crime came to light.

The story of Stanley and his brother sounds somewhat like that of the Biblical Cain and Abel.

Getting Started

1. How would you describe the relationship between Cain and Abel?

2. How would others describe your relationship with your brothers and sisters in the Lord?

Just like Cain

God's children are marked by their obedience and love, but Satan's children do not practice righteousness or love.

3. What are some actions that reveal a lack of love?

From the beginning of Jesus' earthly ministry, New Testament teaching has included the command to love one another (John 13:34, 35). The commandment to love is the old but new commandment John discussed earlier (1 John 2:7–11). God requires that His children love as He loves, so Christians are obligated to love one another.

4. What are some actions that reveal a commitment to godly love?

First John 3:12 presents a stark contrast to the Christian priority on love. It mentions Cain, who demonstrated by his behavior that he was a child of the Devil rather than a child of God.

5. Read Genesis 4:1–15. What factors led to Cain's sin?

6. What effect did Cain's sin have on him and on his family?

7. According to 1 John 3:12, why is Cain considered a child of the Devil?

The Devil's children are characterized by hatred. Cain could not tolerate Abel's righteousness. Rather than change, Cain chose to remove the reminder of his sins. In so doing, he demonstrated that he valued his self-esteem more than justice or love. Cain's hatred was the seed of sin that produced the fruit of murder.

The false teachers in John's day were following Cain's path of hatred and hostility toward the truth. Following them would lead to spiritual disaster.

The sinful world has always been full of those, like Cain, who hate God's righteous people. Because the world is evil, Christians should expect to be mistreated (1 John 3:13).

Mirror to the World

Righteous living that pleases God functions as a mirror to the world. In the lives of Christians, the sinful world can see how it should be living and how far short of God's standard it is. Righteous living makes the world look bad. In fact, the more Christlike a Christian's life, the more he should expect to provoke hostility (2 Timothy 3:12).

8. When has your righteous living provoked a hostile response from an unbeliever?

Because of the inherited sin nature, all people begin life as the children of Satan. But Christians have been born again; their changed practice reflects their changed position (1 John 3:14). By believing in Christ, they have passed from the realm of spiritual death into the realm of spiritual life (John 5:24).

Those who do not demonstrate love reveal that they still abide in

Satan's realm of death. Their lack of love is symptomatic of a deeper spiritual problem. So, the way Christians treat one another is very important. The absence of love is incompatible with the life of Christ (1 John 3:15). Hatred reveals the same corrupt value system that Cain evidenced. In fact, murder is hatred taken to its logical conclusion.

9. In Matthew 5:21 and 22, what correlation did Jesus make between hatred and murder?

Many like to believe that people are basically good. If that were true, love for others would come naturally. But, because of the fall, humans are sinners. By nature, they follow the example of Cain, placing self-interest ahead of righteousness. Their lack of love may not go to his murderous lengths, yet they follow his pattern.

Just like Christ

Christ provides a different and better pattern. According to 1 John 3:16, Christian love is doing unto others as Christ has already done unto you. Christ laid down His life for undeserving people, and that is the pattern believers should follow.

10. Read John 15:13. What kinds of sacrifices can we give every day to show love?

Love is for sharing. Those who have received God's love are indebted to sacrifice themselves for others. Few Christians may be required to actually suffer martyrdom, but all are called to give up personal preferences and prerogatives to put others ahead of themselves.

Christians should demonstrate love by giving what they possess to help others in need. Failure to do so reveals an absence of God's love (1 John 3:17), but genuine Christian love sees and responds to the needs of others. It opens both heart and hand to minister practically. It is sensitive to the point of generous giving. God does not call Christians to give what they do not have, but He does call them to give out of what He has given to them.

11. What are some ways in which Christians can give to meet the needs of others?

Real Christian love is not just words that sound good; it is manifested in action (1 John 3:18). The world has tried its kind of "love" and found it empty and unsatisfying. It waits to see genuine love in the lives of God's children. Only that kind of love truly satisfies.

12. What are some very practical areas of ministry that can evidence true love?

Confidence Threat

The end of 1 John 3:18 exhorts Christians to love in deed and in truth. Verse 19 tells how believers can be assured that they are in the truth, rather than doubting themselves.

Some people teach that doubt itself is sin, yet doubt afflicts all believers periodically.

13. What is doubt?

14. Can doubt be a temptation from Satan? Explain.

15. When does doubt become sin?

Doubt is not denying God, but it involves uncertainty about the reality of a person's relationship with God. Doubt becomes sin when a person chooses to live on the basis of those kinds of fears and refuses to accept the facts that God teaches in Scripture. Such feelings are subjective and prone to error. They must never become the compass for life.

Referring to the previous discussion of love as the mark of the family of God, John showed that love for others is an evidence that a person truly belongs to God. Love does not come naturally to sinners, so its presence reveals that God has worked supernaturally in a person's life. The Christian whose life is marked by love can be confident before God. His fear can be replaced by faith.

Unfortunately, ungrounded doubts can compromise confidence toward God (1 John 3:20). For John's readers, this was precisely what the false teachers threatened to do. Their teaching was introducing questions and fears that caused Christians to wonder if they truly belonged to God.

16. What happens to a believer's spiritual growth when he begins to doubt his salvation?

Whenever negative feelings threaten a Christian's confidence, one thing is certain: God knows the truth about His children. His knowledge is not clouded by human fears. He knows His children perfectly, so any doubts they have are unfounded. Confidence comes from trusting the facts, not feelings or opinions.

Confidence in Prayer

Christians can have confidence before God. This confidence is openness to approach God boldly, particularly in prayer (1 John 3:21).

The false teachers had prompted doubts that caused Christians to be hesitant toward God. When doubt is not dealt with, it can easily turn into despair. John did not want Christians to become paralyzed by their feelings. Neither did he encourage them to deny the existence of their doubts. Ignoring doubt is self-deception, not an indicator of genuine faith.

Instead, John wanted to show the way to true confidence and bold-ness before God. This comes only when doubts are faced honestly and answered in terms of the truth. Believers need to evaluate themselves as God does if they are to be confident before Him.

17. What might hinder a Christian from performing such honest evaluation?

Confidence for Christians comes when their lives evidence the marks of obedience and love (1 John 3:22). When Christians are obey-ing God's commandments and doing what pleases Him, then they can boldly present their requests before Him.

As a loving Father, God delights to answer His children's requests (Matthew 7:7–11). At the same time, as a wise Father He also knows what is best for them. This is not an unconditional guarantee that God will always give what His children request. But it is a general principle that the more a Christian does what delights the Father, the more that believer will desire and request what God wants to give him.

First 1 John 3:23 spells out one of the things that delight the Father. It is stated as a single commandment with two dimensions: vertical and horizontal. The vertical dimension is to believe on the name of Jesus Christ. The horizontal dimension is to love one another. Here the Chris-tian life is boiled down to its essential ingredients: love the Lord your God, and love your neighbor.

The false teachers fell short in both areas. They substituted false be-lief and false behavior. God's commandment demands true belief, genu-ine love, and faithful obedience.

However, keeping God's commandments is not simply a matter of deciding to do what is right. Because of inherited sin, we cannot obey God's commands apart from the power of the indwelling Holy Spirit (3:24). The one who obeys God's commands evidences that he abides in Christ and that Christ abides in him. When a person accepts Christ, the Holy Spirit comes to live within him. The Spirit produces His righteous fruit (Galatians 5:22, 23), which includes love and faith.

Those who walk in the Spirit can see what He is producing in their lives, and that provides them with confidence that they truly are God's people.

Making It Personal

18. Examine your life in light of the following concepts from 1 John 3, and write a prayer in response.

> • How Christians treat one another is very important. The absence of love (hatred) is incompatible with the life of Christ.

> • Christian love goes well beyond the golden rule. Christian love is doing unto others as Christ has already done unto us.

> • True confidence and boldness before God comes only when doubts are faced honestly and answered in terms of the truth.

19. Later this week, review your prayer and these concepts. Use them to renew your mind.

20. Memorize 1 John 3:16.

Discerning Truth and Error

Christians must be careful to discern between truth and error.

1 John 4:1–6

"Hereby know ye the Spirit of God: Every spirit that confesseth that Jesus Christ is come in the flesh is of God" (1 John 4:2).

Loupe, binocular microscope, refractometer, dischroscope, polariscope—they don't sound the least bit romantic. But before a man buys a gem for his best girl, he'll want to make sure it has been tested by one of these scientific instruments. In the past, before synthetic stones were created and perfected, experts could tell the fake from the genuine with a good eye or a good magnifying glass. No more! Now such discernment requires those fine instruments with their funny-sounding names.

No woman wants to learn that her man gave her a cheap substitute for the real thing. Believers, too, want the real thing when they look for a church. They don't want a fake that looks good on the outside but has no genuine worth because it does not hold to the entire Bible.

Getting Started

1. If you were new in a community, how would you begin looking for a church while at the same time avoiding spiritual deception?

2. What could your church do to help people looking for a church understand your doctrinal stand?

Searching the Scriptures

The Test of Affirmation

In today's world, one of the highest values is tolerance. Christians certainly should treat others with kindness, even if their beliefs differ from the Christian faith. This kind of thoughtful regard, however, is not what contemporary proponents of toleration demand. Instead, by "tolerance" they mean that all beliefs are equally valid and that it is wrong to insist that one is superior to another.

Although John taught that love for others is a distinguishing mark of genuine Christians, he clearly opposed the modern notion of tolerance. He challenged his readers not to believe every spirit, but to test the spirits to determine if they were truly of God. This is not tolerance in the modern sense of unthinking acceptance of contradictory views; it is careful evaluation of all claims in light of God's truth.

Throughout history many false teachers have proclaimed their beliefs as representative of God's truth. They may sound attractive and seem sincere—even appearing very spiritual. However, not everything that represents itself as from God truly is. Not everything that is "spiritual" finds its source in the Holy Spirit. Because of this, John insisted that all spiritual claims be examined to determine if they are genuinely from God.

3. What spiritual claims have you come across that seemed plausible until you learned more about them?

By instructing the Christians to "try the spirits whether they are of God," John was not encouraging Christians to have a harsh attitude that delights in putting others down. Christians are often accused of this kind of spirit, and unfortunately sometimes the criticism is deserved.

John wanted Christians to think clearly and to see through attractive language to discern the true facts. Being godly should not mean being gullible. Discerning Christians are not overly impressed by appearances and carefully evaluate all claims to determine if they correspond to Scripture.

Giving a religious teacher this kind of scrutiny should not be viewed as insulting. In fact, a true Biblical teacher should welcome it.

4. Read Acts 17:11. How did the Bereans respond to the teachings of Paul and Silas?

5. How can you develop a critical mind without having a critical spirit?

Nature of the Test

First John 4:2 states a clear standard for evaluating spiritual teachers. Those who truly represent the Spirit of God confess that Jesus has come in the flesh. Those who deny that fundamental fact are not speaking truth.

In the early church many false doctrines were proclaimed. Typically these erroneous teachings failed to hold to the Biblical teaching about Christ. Some false teachers claimed that Jesus only seemed to be human but that in reality He was deity without a human nature. Others said

Jesus was adopted by God after the crucifixion so that at that time He became the Son of God.

6. Why are the teachings that Jesus was never human or that He became the Son of God after the crucifixion incompatible with the gospel?

The New Testament teaches clearly that Jesus Christ was eternally the Son of God. In the Incarnation, the Son of God became flesh (John 1:14, 18). From the time that Jesus was born, He was fully human and fully divine. That unique combination qualified Him to die on the cross as the sinless substitute for humans, fully satisfying God's righteous demands.

This doctrine of the God-man is a nonnegotiable essential of the Christian faith. The false teachers in the first century denied this doctrine. Much religious talk today speaks only of a generic God without reference to Christ. This falls short of the standard of 1 John 4:2. God's truth always exalts Christ.

7. How can we distinguish between true Christians from a different denominational background and false teachers engaged in serious error?

News of the Test

8. What does 1 John 4:3 call the spirit that does not confess that Jesus Christ came in the flesh?

Any teaching that rejects or downplays the deity or humanity of Jesus Christ is false, and does not come from God—no matter how attractively it may be presented or how well-intentioned the teacher may seem.

9. In your estimation, how widespread is such false teaching about Christ?

If the teaching is not of God, then it must originate elsewhere. False teaching comes ultimately from the spirit of antichrist. Religious language that does not honor Jesus as the incarnate Son of God is an imitation that seeks to replace God's genuine truth. In devaluing Christ, it is actually opposing Him. Any teacher that diminishes the person of Christ is antichrist. In other words, "antichrist" refers to the whole class of false teachers that will culminate in the final Antichrist of the tribulation period.

The continuing existence of the spirit of antichrist requires that Christians be vigilant. They must look beyond appearances to discern how teachings compare with the fixed standard of God's truth.

The Test of Acceptance

Throughout 1 John, John reassured his readers that they truly belonged to God. To alleviate their concerns raised by the false teachers, John reminded them, "Ye are of God, little children" (4:4). Whatever they may have thought, John was convinced that they were truly children of God. They needed to remember that reality in the face of the false teachers' attacks.

10. Why would remembering they belong to God be helpful to them?

John also reminded the Christians of their past conflicts with error (4:4). The false teachings that threatened them were nothing new. In the past they had overcome similar attacks on their faith. They were victorious in seeing through the false claims and overcoming them by the truth.

Above all, they could be confident because God's superior power was available to them. The false teachers could be clever, persuasive, and even intimidating, but God is more than sufficient to counteract every threat. Christians do not have to face the challenge alone; in God's power and wisdom they can prevail (4:4).

Ultimately all false teaching finds its source in Satan. Sometimes Christians speak and think of Satan as God's equal. However, the Bible teaches that Satan is a created being who is infinitely beneath God in power and intelligence. There are not two equal deities, one good and the other evil. Satan, despite his strategies and efforts, is unable to match God.

11. How can we refute the false teaching that Satan is the evil counterpart to God?

Since God is greater than Satan, He is certainly greater than the false teachers who work under Satan's direction. Christians are on the victor's side and need not live defeated lives, but should live like the winners they will be.

No Acceptance by the World

In 2:15–17, John contrasted the world with God the Father. He warned Christians not to love the world because if anyone does, then love for the Father is not in him. Both the world and God insist on total allegiance and devotion.

John stated emphatically that the false teachers were part of the world system that is aligned against God. False teaching today often lifts its subject matter and approaches from contemporary life. By speaking in the dialect of contemporary society, it is able to grab attention and get a hearing. The world is often much more open to a version of its own story than it is to gospel story. As a result, the world often finds false teaching attractive when it will not consider traditional Christianity. By adopting the world's style, false teaching gains an entrance that the truth is not given.

12. What are some examples of false teachings that are attractive to the world?

13. In what ways have you noticed false teaching gaining an entrance in school classrooms and public workplaces today?

To a certain extent, Christians must present the gospel in terms that are relevant to their culture. Nevertheless, if the gospel of Christ is diluted to make it acceptable to the world, then the world is not hearing truth, but a pale imitation of it. The world should not dictate what Christians believe, how they behave, or what they proclaim. In their faith, action, and witness Christians must conform to the Word, not to the world.

14. How can Christians be effective witnesses without compromising with the culture?

Jesus warned His disciples in John 15:18–23 that the world loves its own but hates those who belong to God. John applied that warning to the evaluation of spiritual teaching. If the world loves it, then it likely finds its source in the world. If the teaching is truly of God, then the world will reject it. According to Scripture, one can discern much about a teacher by the friends he keeps and the enemies he makes.

Acceptance of the Truth

In contrast to the antichrists, the apostles were of God (1 John 4:6). They were children of God through faith in Christ. Additionally, God was the source of their message. Their teaching was genuine and reliable.

Just as the world accepted those who were of the world (4:5), so those who know God will accept the truth as declared by the apostles (4:6). They recognize God's truth when they hear it because they know God, the author of truth.

15. What does it mean to accept God's truth?

Those who do not have a relationship with God are unable to hear and accept His truth. Paul taught in 1 Corinthians 2:14 that the unsaved person cannot accept the things of the Spirit of God, because they seem foolish to him. Spiritual truth can be understood only by those who know God and His indwelling Spirit.

16. What has happened when you have tried to explain God's truth to an unbeliever?

Those who are of the world will be attracted to false teaching, because it speaks their language. Those who are of God will appreciate God's truth as it is proclaimed by His genuine spokespersons.

Making It Personal

17. What is your attitude toward those who promote false teachings?

18. How do you pray for them? How should you pray for them?

Instead of gullibly believing everyone, we need to think clearly, observe carefully, and choose wisely whom we will believe and follow.

19. What are you watching or listening to that deserves a critical look?

20. What might be having a negative impact on your life spiritually?

21. Memorize 1 John 4:2.

Love Is of God

*Godly love is demonstrated by love
and care for others.*

1 John 4:7–21

**"And we have known and believed the love
that God hath to us. God is love; and he that
dwelleth in love dwelleth in God, and God in
him" (1 John 4:16).**

They stood second-to-last in line to greet and be photo-graphed with U.S. Rep. Gabrielle Giffords. That's when seventeen-year-old Emma McMahon learned just how much her mother, Mary Reed, loves her. Hearing a loud, bad sound, Mary pushed Emma against a brick wall and blanketed herself around her daughter. Thud. The first of three bullets struck Mary. Although wounded and terrified, Mary did not move. She would not expose Emma to the danger.

Emma was left unhurt, and Mary survived to tell her story. But not everyone who demonstrates sacrificial love in such a dramatic way does survive. And everyone who gives sacrificial love does not do so in such a dramatic way. Sacrificial love can be a part of everyday life.

Getting Started

1. Describe how someone showed love to you in a sacrificial way.

2. How have you loved someone sacrificially?

Searching the Scriptures

Pattern for Love

Several times John addressed his readers as "beloved." With this af-fectionate title he was expressing his love, even though he taught stern-ly. As he challenged them to demonstrate the mark of Christian love, he reassured them of their position in God's family. They were beloved to him and to God.

In 1 John 4:7 John included himself in the exhortation: "Let us love one another." The threat of error could easily have dominated his read-ers' attention so that they lost focus on loving one another. Even an apostle like John could become distracted from love, so he made the exhortation applicable to all.

3. How can we keep love and discernment in balance?

Verse 8 states that failure to love reveals that a person does not know God. Love finds its source and perfect expression in God alone. Therefore, if a person does not practice love, there is evidence that he does not know God.

The Greek language used several terms to speak of love. The word *epithumia* referred to self-seeking desire; *eros*, to emotional passion and physical intimacy. *Storge* is the love of loyal devotion; *philia* is reliable friendship. All these aspects of love have importance, but John challenged Christians to the higher standard of *agape* love. God's *agape* love is vol-untary action to help someone in need, despite the cost. It is uncondi-tional love that asks what it can give, not get. In this aspect of love, God alone is the perfect example. His pattern is the standard for His children.

4. Read 1 John 4:9. Why is God the perfect example of *agape* love?

Christ entered the human race so He could die on the cross as the perfect substitute for all sinners, thus offering them life. In this action people learn the essence of genuine love (1 John 4:9, 10). God's love took the initiative to help humans in need. Instead of gratifying itself, God's love gave. His love was not conditional, but was freely and unconditionally extended even to those who were totally unworthy. God's love valued the life it could give above the cost it would require.

5. What does God's example of love teach you about how you are to love?

God took the initiative to love sinners despite their condition. He sent His Son to earth to become human and die on the cross. By doing this, Christ was the propitiation, or legal satisfaction for the wrath of God. Through the death of His Son, God reconciled sinners to Himself. His love did for us what we could never do ourselves. By giving His Son, God demonstrated *agape* in its perfect form—costly sacrifice to help those in need.

Christians have experienced God's love to them in the gift of salvation through the death of Christ. Because they have freely received God's love, they are under obligation to reach out to others with the same sacrificial love (4:11). John challenged Christians to do unto others as God had done unto them. Those who appreciate God's love should be channels of it to others.

6. What are some reasons we might not show *agape* love as we ought?

Perfection of Love

Parents typically have high aspirations for their children. As a Father, God wants His children to become like Jesus. He works toward that goal in their lives to perfect His love in them.

Christ came and demonstrated to the world what God the Father is like (John 1:18). Now God represents Himself to the world through believers, particularly through their love (1 John 4:12). What the watching world understands about God is directly related to what it sees in Christians. If the world does not see love in their lives, its view of God is distorted.

7. Will we always know how the world views us as Christians? Explain.

How can people really know if they are dwelling in God, and He in them? That is the fundamental question that John answered in this letter. First John contains three marks that characterize the live of true Christians—love, obedience, and truth. The cumulative testimony of these witnesses provides confidence before God.

Love is a mark of the Christian because it is the fruit produced by the Holy Spirit (4:13)—Who is God's gift to His children (1 John 3:24).

8. Read 1 John 4:13. If love is produced by the Holy Spirit, are believers still responsible to show it? Explain.

John consistently linked love and truth (4:14). The apostles were eyewitnesses of Christ's death and had personally seen the evidence that Jesus was the Son of God (John 20:30, 31). In addition to the inner conviction of the Spirit, they had seen the objective, historical evidence of Jesus' claims. They witnessed God's love in action as they watched Jesus die on the cross. John had no doubt about who Jesus was or what He came to do.

First John 4:12 states that God dwells in those who love one another. Verse 15 says that God dwells in those who confess that Jesus is the Son of God. These two statements evidence that love and truth are complementary, not contrasting. God's children are characterized by both right behavior and right belief. God's presence teaches them to know the truth and practice love.

9. What might happen if believers emphasize truth at the expense of love as they witness?

10. What might happen if believers emphasize love at the expense of truth as they witness?

John's insistence on right belief about the Person of Christ reveals that if a person is wrong about Jesus, he cannot be right with God. False teaching about Christ stems only from ungodly, unreliable teachers.

Speaking of himself and the readers, John said: "We have known and believed the love that God hath to us" (4:16). Such love was the gift of His Son (John 3:16).

As the Spirit produces His fruit of love in believers, that love becomes evidence that they are indeed dwelling in God.

11. Read 1 John 4:17. What will God's love in you do for you as you stand before the Judgment Seat of Christ?

The New Testament teaches that Christians will appear before Christ to answer for how they have lived (2 Corinthians 5:10). First John 2:28 exhorts Christians to abide in Christ so that they will have boldness, not shame, at His return.

When God's love is perfected in His children, their lives become increasingly pleasing to Him. Instead of living by their natural selfish desires, they are moved by God's love toward selfless, sacrificial love for others. Perfected love keeps God's Word (1 John 2:5). Consequently, when the Christian appears before Christ, he can have confidence that Christ will approve his life, for it has been marked by love and obedience.

12. How can you improve your confidence about appearing before Christ?

Love that has been brought to completion casts out fear about appearing before Christ (4:18). The person who fears standing before Christ is the one who has displeased God, because he has not loved others. His lack of love evidences a problem in his relationship with God, and that affects his attitude toward appearing before Christ. Like a child dreading disapproval from his parent, so Christians who are not living up to their spiritual potential in loving others will experience fear rather than confidence before God.

Practice of Love

13. Rate yourself on how well you think you show love to your fellow believers. Write a number based on a scale of 1 to 4; with 1 representing "sacrificial and personal" and 4 representing "indifferent and careless."

14. Now rate how well members of your church do at showing love to others.

15. How are the two ratings connected?

John concluded this extended challenge to love by reemphasizing the practice of love. For Christians, love is not an option, but an obligation. Love is not just a general principle for consideration, but it involves specific practice. Those who claim to love God must demonstrate godly love toward others.

Among the earliest Greek manuscripts, some copies of 1 John 4:19 read, "We love him [God], because he first loved us," but others read, "We love, because he first loved us." The former reading focuses on how our love for God is a response to His love for us in Christ. The latter reading emphasizes that Christians have the capacity to love one another because God has first extended His love to them.

Both of these readings are theologically accurate. In addition, 1 John teaches both of them. In either case, the point is clear: those who say that they love God must love their fellow Christians.

16. Read 1 John 4:20. If a person truly loves God, why must he love his fellow believers too?

Love does not come naturally, because people are born with an inherited sin nature that drives them toward selfishness. Only God's love can prompt a response of love. God is the power and pattern of believers' love for Him and for one another.

It is easy to say, "I love God," but the proof of that love is in how a person treats others (4:20). Love for God cannot coexist with hatred for others. In fact, love for the invisible God is visibly demonstrated by love for one another. As John taught in 2:9, hating others is walking in the darkness of disobedience.

17. Can Christians be tempted to hate? What is the proper response?

Verse 20 teaches that Christians should do unto others as they would do unto Christ. This reminds us of Jesus' teaching in Matthew

25:31–46, when He said, "Inasmuch as ye have done it unto one of the least of these my brethren, ye have done it unto me" (25:40). How Christians treat others is extremely important to God.

First John 4:21 restates Christ's new commandment "that he who loveth God love his brother also" (4:21). Once again 1 John emphasizes that love for others is God's command.

Christians do not have the luxury of choosing whether or not to love others. They are as obligated to love others as they are to love God Himself.

Making It Personal

18. Can believers show a sacrificial, personal love to others if they do not know them personally? Why? How?

19. How can believers develop relationships that would encourage such personal love in action?

20. Select at least one person to love sacrificially and personally this week.

21. Memorize 1 John 4:16.

Faith That Overcomes

Faith in Christ overcomes the world.

1 John 5:1–12

"For whatsoever is born of God overcometh the world: and this is the victory that overcometh the world, even our faith" (1 John 5:4).

In the middle of the last century, a family found a box of metal teeth in their attic. Their dentist-ancestor had kept on hand a number of sets. A patient would come in, and the dentist would find the set that best fit that patient. Eventually he no longer needed those inexpensive false teeth and junked them in a box in the attic. The family who found the box were going to throw it away until someone suggested they take the teeth to a jeweler to identify the metal. By then, platinum had become expensive, and each set of teeth sold for $300. The family made $8,000 from that box of junk. And that was at 1950s prices! Imagine what those platinum false teeth would fetch today!

Getting Started

1. What is the most valuable item you have ever discovered you owned?

2. What did you do once you discovered the item?

One of John's purposes in this letter was to help Christians realize their riches in Christ. As the false teachers were endeavoring to undermine their faith in Christ, John wrote to reinforce it. By reminding them of the consequences of their faith, John wanted to renew their commitment to Christ.

Faith Leads to Obedience

First John 5:1 states that whoever believes that Jesus is the Christ has been born of God. The false teachers rejected Jesus as the incarnate Son of God, demonstrating that they were not in God's family.

On the other hand, the recipients of 1 John did believe in Christ, indicating that they had been born again into God's family through faith (John 1:12).

Christians have become God's spiritual children. They cannot truly love the Father without also loving His family. The implication is clear: those who do not love God's children place a question mark over the reality of their love for God Himself.

3. How do parents show their children how to love?

4. According to 1 John 5:2 and 3, how do God's children learn to love one another?

Within human families, loving parents show children how to love. By their pattern of love they demonstrate how their children should act toward others. Likewise, God has demonstrated His love to His children so that they might see His quality of love in action and then imitate it.

Loving parents also teach principles of loving behavior. Similarly,

God has set forth commandments that teach His children how to treat others. Those who adopt God's instructions learn to practice love for others as they follow those instructions.

5. Which of God's commands for believers today are related to their love for others?

At times, loving others goes against what Christians feel and desire. For godly love is not limited by feelings but is obedient to God's commandment. Christians have the obligation to love others as God does— especially when it goes against what they want to do. In this way, they evidence the presence of the Spirit of God in their lives. Their relationship with God empowers them to love in a supernatural way.

Verse 3 clearly states the relationship between love and obedience: loving God equals keeping His commandments. This was precisely what Jesus said in John 14:15: "If ye love me, keep my commandments." This may sound strange to us, because to our minds love and law seem to be nearly opposite. Yet God's love and His law both come from His perfect nature.

God's laws actually grow out of His love, even as parents make rules for children because they love them and want to protect them. God is not an arbitrary despot who makes unreasonable demands. Rather, His laws are for the good of His children, because they lead to blessing and fullness of life.

6. What rules did your parents set up for you that particularly demonstrated their love for you?

By commanding love, God is challenging believers to practice the kinds of actions and attitudes that will better their lives and the lives of others. His commands are not a burden, but are the path to real life and joy. God wants the very best for the children He loves. If believers truly love their Father, they will do as He directs, finding the way of blessing.

7. Why do God's commands sometimes *seem* burdensome?

Faith Brings Victory

In addition to obeying the Lord, those who have become God's children by faith in Christ are able to overcome the world (1 John 5:4).

The world is tempting and powerful, and it is able to control unsaved people. God's children, however, have a spiritual resource that empowers them. They are not helpless before the onslaught of the world. They need not succumb to its pressures.

8. Read 1 John 5:4 and 5. What does it mean to overcome the world?

9. Have you ever had a time when you thought overcoming the world was impossible? What contributed to that mindset?

Even though the world may seem invincible at times, it is no match for God. His omnipotence is more than able to conquer it. His omniscience can see through its clever deceptions.

God makes His victory over the world available to all of His children. Spiritual victory is not a limited privilege for the spiritually elite; it is promised to all who are born of God.

The world is already passing away (2:17). Christ broke its power when He died on the cross, and God "delivered us from the power of darkness, and hath translated us into the kingdom of his dear Son" (Colossians 1:13). Those who are in Christ are on the victorious side in the conflict with the world. Through faith in Christ they no longer are compelled to follow the world's dictates. Against the full range of evil's assaults, God's children can stand their ground.

10. How can your faith in Christ give you victory over the world?

Christians must maintain faith in Christ on an ongoing basis to experience continued victory over the world. It is the object of faith, not the quantity of faith, that is all-important. Victory does not come through confidence in one's own intelligence, ability, or experience. Even a great amount of that kind of confidence can lead to spiritual defeat. On the other hand, just a mustard seed of faith in Christ is sufficient to meet any challenges that the world can pose.

This truth is reaffirmed in verse 5. Only those who believe that Jesus is the Son of God are able to overcome the world. Christ conquered the world on the cross, so faith in Him gives victory over the world.

11. What will happen if we place confidence in self instead of in Christ?

Confidence of Faith

First John 5:6 and 8 identifies three witnesses that testify to the legitimacy of faith in Christ. The first witness is the Holy Spirit. As 1 Corinthians 2:10 teaches, the Spirit knows even "the deep things of God" and reveals them to Christians. The Spirit always teaches the truth, and He witnesses to the fact that Jesus is the Christ, the Son of God (5:6).

12. How does the Spirit teach us?

The false teachers of John's day, specifically Cerinthus, claimed that Jesus became the Christ at His baptism and that the divine Christ left the human Jesus at the Crucifixion. In other words, they said that the Son of God participated in the water of baptism but that He did not participate in the blood of the cross.

The apostle John, speaking by the inspiration of the Holy Spirit, contradicted the error of Cerinthus and other false teachers. Jesus Christ was the Son of God who took on human flesh in the incarnation (John 1:1–14). Throughout His entire earthly ministry—and continuing forever—Jesus was the unique God-man. He did not die as a mere man, but as the incarnate Son of God. Because of that, He has taken the place of sinful humans and has completely met the righteous demands of the holy God. Faith in Christ, then, is securely grounded, so Christians can be confident in it.

Verse 8 returns to the point begun in verse 6. According to Deuteronomy 19:15, three witnesses were sufficient to establish a fact in a court of law. First John 5:8 points to the Spirit, the baptism of Christ, and the crucifixion of Christ as witnesses to Christ as the incarnate Son of God. The inner testimony of the Holy Spirit (Romans 8:16), the audible voice at Christ's baptism (Matthew 3:17), and the physical phenomena at the crucifixion (Mark 15:39) all point to the same conclusion.

This evidence gives Christians overwhelming confidence about their faith in Jesus, even in the face of false teaching.

13. What are some evidences that a believer is putting his faith in Christ for spiritual victory?

14. What are some signs that a person might be putting his faith in himself for spiritual victory?

Superior Witness

People customarily make decisions based upon trusted evidence.

God's witness about Christ is ultimate and self-authenticating (1 John 5:9). God's testimony about His Son is sufficient. Faith is accepting it as reliable and acting on that basis by believing in Christ.

Faith takes God at His Word rather than considering that word to be inferior to human claims.

15. Read 1 John 5:9 and 10. Why is God's witness about Jesus Christ sufficient?

Accepting God's testimony produces belief in Christ (5:10). Refusing to believe in Christ is tantamount to calling God a liar. By rejecting His testimony, a believer is considering God an untrustworthy witness.

God's Word cannot be measured by any other standard. People must believe that what He says is true simply because He said it.

16. Why can God's Word not be measured by any other standard?

Christians believe God's Word, not just when it makes sense to them or when they have independent confirmation from another source. To disbelieve any part of the Bible is sinful refusal to trust the Word of the Lord.

Sustaining Witness

17. What is the testimony in 1 John 5:11 and 12?

Verse 11 expands on the record that God gave of His Son. God has testified that He has given eternal life, and that it comes only through His Son. Just as the Holy Spirit bears witness to Jesus Christ (5:6), so, too, does God the Father. The Godhead is united in confirming that Jesus is the Christ—God the Son.

Various religions have taught different ways to please God or gain eternal life. The Bible rejects the notion that all these religious paths lead to God. People need more than sincerity in their beliefs; they need the Savior for their sins. Jesus stated in John 14:6 that He alone is the way to God and that no one comes to the Father except through Him.

This truth is reinforced in 1 John 5:12, which makes an unmistakable distinction between those who believe in Christ and those who do not. The one who has the Son has life, but the one who does not have the Son does not have life. Belief in Jesus and eternal life are inseparable.

18. When have you encountered someone who was sincere about a false religion? How did you respond?

As Christians face challenges and opposition from the world, they can stand firmly on the fact that God has given to them eternal life in Christ. Their faith provides a relationship with God and life from Him that will never end.

Making It Personal

19. Whom or what do you put your faith in when you face spiritual battles? How do you know?

20. Have you been trusting in yourself for spiritual victory? If so, write out a prayer dealing with the matter before the Lord.

21. How often do you go to God with your spiritual battles? Commit to placing your faith in Christ for victory.

22. Memorize 1 John 5:4.

Confidence in the Face of Conflict

Confidence for life comes from knowing Christ.

1 John 5:13–21

"And we know that the Son of God is come, and hath given us an understanding, that we may know him that is true, and we are in him that is true, even in his Son Jesus Christ. This is the true God, and eternal life" (1 John 5:20).

A self-help guru says that if you want your boss to notice you among his other employees, you can't just do your job well. You have to gain his confidence, to let him know "you are the one person who can be trusted and relied on." This expert gives three simple tips: be punctual, be courteous, and be honest. Since these qualities should characterize Christians anyway, it seems that bosses, and others, would very easily place their confidence in them.

Getting Started

1. Who has won your confidence?

2. How did they earn it?

3. How does your level of confidence in a person affect the way you interact with that person?

John ended his epistle by talking about confidence. He wanted his readers to be assured of what they had learned from him through the letter. Confidence in Christ is foundational to a growing relationship with Him. The false teachers threatened to destroy that confidence and thereby cause the believers to live stagnant spiritual lives.

Searching the Scriptures

Confidence of Eternal Life

4. According to 1 John 5:13, how important is the confidence of eternal life to you? Is there anything that compares to it?

The Gospel of John was designed to convince people to believe in Christ (John 20:30, 31). First John was written to people who had already believed in Christ but were struggling with doubt. The Gospel of John was designed for evangelism, while the Epistle focuses on encouragement.

The false teachers had tried to undermine faith in Christ. Their attacks had provoked confusion and doubt in the minds of believers. John did not dismiss the doubts as insignificant fears. Rather, he addressed the issues that the false teachers raised. In doing this, John wanted to close the gap between the believers' confession and their confidence. He wanted to remind them of their faith in Christ, to reassure them of their position in Christ, and to rebuild their confidence in Christ.

5. Have you struggled with assurance of salvation in the past? What helped you gain confidence of eternal life?

One of the key terms John used was "know." As he looked back to the whole letter, and in particular to what he had just written in 5:9–12, John said that he had written these things to believers in Christ so that they would know that they have eternal life on the basis of their faith. This life is a present reality that only God's children enjoy.

In seeking to undermine belief in Christ, false teachers were casting doubt on the future of those who trusted in Him. Those who are uncertain about their future find it hard to be confident in the present. By reassuring them that they had eternal life in Christ, John rebuilt their confidence in the face of conflict. That confidence could give them stability in the struggles of life.

6. How can the confidence of eternal life give strength to stand in life's struggles?

Confidence for Prayer

7. Read 1 John 5:14 and 15. How important is confidence for prayer to you?

One of the great benefits Christians have is the assurance that they can go directly to God in prayer. As Hebrews 4:16 teaches, Christ has opened the way for His people to "come boldly unto the throne of grace, that [they] may obtain mercy, and find grace to help in time of need."

8. Why can believers have confidence when they pray (1 John 5:14)?

The confidence that Christians can have as they pray is not based in their own worthiness or related to their skill in knowing what words to say. Rather, confidence in prayer is rooted in the faithful character of God, Who promises to hear (5:14).

When Jesus prayed to the Father in the Garden of Gethsemane, He said, "Thy will be done" (Matthew 26:42). For Christians to pray in confidence, they, too, must ask according to God's will. In prayer, believers surrender their will to God's perfect will. Prayer is not demanding that God do as they desire, but asking God to do what is best.

Just as loving parents want their children to be honest in presenting their requests and sharing their desires, so the Father wants His children to approach Him openly and candidly. Nevertheless, loving parents do not always do what their children ask. They may know better what is in the best interests of their children. At such times, children need to trust their parents' loving wisdom even when their requests are not granted. In an even greater way, Christians can be certain that God hears their prayers. He knows what is best for them and will do even more than what they have requested.

Verse 15 reinforces this truth. God does hear and respond to the prayers of His people.

9. In light of this promise, how should believers respond?

Prayer is not the way in which God gets information that He otherwise would not know. Being omniscient, He already fully knows what each of His children faces, needs, and wants. But prayer is God's designated means for accomplishing His purposes. Christians pray because God has commanded them to. How prayer accomplishes His sovereign purpose is beyond human comprehension. God does His perfect will at His perfect time in His perfect way. Believers cannot dictate the terms to God. At the same time, because God has directed that His children come to Him in prayer, they must never underestimate its significance. As James 5:16 teaches, "The effectual fervent prayer of a righteous man availeth much."

One of the great privileges that God's children have is to come openly to the Father to present their requests, knowing that He wants to hear and help.

10. How can confidence for prayer give strength to stand in life's struggles?

Confidence about Sin

Christians can and do sin. Instead of denying that possibility, they need to examine their lives and be aware of the spiritual needs of one another.

11. What kind of prayer should we pray for a Christian who has sinned (5:16)?

When Christians observe a brother or sister in Christ who has sinned, they need to pray for God to restore that person. Christians who have prepared themselves by prayer should seek to restore that person "in the spirit of meekness" (Galatians 6:1).

12. What sinful responses do believers sometimes have when other believers sin?

The sin unto death is deliberate refusal to believe in Christ (1 John 5:16). Such rejection of Christ places a person outside the sphere of eternal life. John 3:18 states, "He that believeth on him is not condemned: but he that believeth not is condemned already, because he hath not believed in the name of the only begotten Son of God."

First John 5:16 clearly teaches that Christians should not pray regarding the sin unto death. Does that mean they should not pray for the salvation of unbelievers? No. It means that it is improper to ask God to lower His requirement of belief in Christ for salvation. That would demean God's grace after He has already paid the ultimate price—the death of His Son. John warned his readers against asking God to contradict His nature by requesting special terms for someone who rejects Christ.

All unbelievers ultimately commit the sin unto death by refusing to believe in Christ. Genuine Christians cannot commit the sin unto death, because they have already believed.

Verse 17 adds that just because a sin will not lead to eternal judgment does not make it acceptable for Christians to commit that sin. Those who are saved are not to please themselves with sin. Sin is any violation of God's righteous standard. All sin breaks God's law and will, and must be confessed and forsaken—even by Christians. The person who has been born into God's family does not lead a life characterized by sin (5:18).

Verse 18 also points out that Christ guards true believers so that Satan cannot harm them. God's children are safely protected, so they can be confident, even when tempted to sin (cf. John 10:27–29; Jude 24).

13. How can confidence about sin give strength to stand in life's struggles?

Confidence in Christ

First John 5:19 reiterates the clear distinction between those who belong to God and those who belong to the world, which lies under satanic control. Even though Christ died for the sins of the whole world (2:2)—His death being sufficient to cover the sins of the human race—not all have accepted that gift. Only those who have received Christ have been born into God's family. All Christians belong to that group. As John said, "We know that we are of God," but outside God's family, the rest of the world lies in the realm of the evil one.

First John 5:20 focuses on the Person of Jesus Christ.

14. Why would 1 John end with this reminder about the true understanding of Christ?

The false teachers had spoken error that led to misunderstanding. Jesus Christ, the incarnate Son of God, came to give true understanding. Only through Christ can fallen people understand what is true and receive eternal life.

The expression "the Son of God is come" in verse 20 refers back to

4:2 and 3. By coming to earth and taking upon Himself human flesh, Christ revealed God's truth (Hebrews 1:1–3).

First John 5:19 and 20 together show that those who truly belong to God have an accurate understanding of Who Christ is. The false teachers were wrong about Christ and did not belong to God. Those who know that Christ is the Son of God and believe in Him are in God's family. As they face life's challenges, their confidence is rooted ultimately in their knowledge of Christ.

15. How can confidence in Christ give strength to stand in life's struggles?

Confidence against Error

First John 5:21 urges Christians to keep themselves from idols. God always protects His children, but they must do their part by maintaining their allegiance to Him. To stand confidently against error, Christians must stay with God and submit to Him. If they are careless, they may find spiritual disaster ready to pounce on them.

When John warned his readers to keep themselves from idols, he had at least two things in mind. In the first-century world, the worship of material images was still an important part of popular religion. The intellectual class had, for the most part, abandoned serious devotion to the old Greek and Roman gods, but the lives of the common people still revolved around idolatry. John, then, was warning Christians not to revert to the idolatry of their pre-Christian lives.

Idols can also be all rival claimants to the worship that belongs to Christ. A deficient view of Christ is essentially the substitution of a human creation for God's truth. The immaterial idols of false doctrine are just as erroneous as material images of gold, silver, and wood. They are all frauds that lead people away from belief in Jesus Christ.

16. Why are all believers vulnerable to false teachings?

17. What are some means by which Christians may resist false doctrine?

Even today, God's people must be on their guard against idolatry. God calls them to complete allegiance to Christ. Anything less than that is idolatry, because it sets Christ in a secondary place. When things like possessions, leisure, amusements, or reputation become more important than living for Christ, idolatry has taken over in the heart.

Satan is crafty in his strategies to deflect attention away from Christ. He uses whatever means he can to set up rivals to take the place of the true worship of Christ. Only by renewing their commitment to Christ can God's children confidently keep themselves against error.

Making It Personal

18. In which of these four areas (eternal life, prayer, sin, and Christ) has your confidence been bolstered the most by this study of 1 John?

19. Write a prayer about any lack of confidence you have.

20. Add to the prayer above, talking to God about growing in the three marks of a Christian: obedience, love, and truth.

21. Memorize 1 John 5:20.